Six Months *In* Captivity In Djibouti, Africa

How God Made a Way of Escape

Lynette Mutembezi

Six Months In Capitivity In Djibouti, Africa : How God Made a Way of Escape
Copyright © 2020 by Lynette Mutembezi.

All rights reserved. Printed in the United States of America. No part of this book may be used or reproduced in any manner whatsoever without written permission except in the case of brief quotations em- bodied in critical articles or reviews.

Publishined by :
Relentless Publishing House
www.relentelesspublishign.com

ISBN: 978-1-948829-84-7

TABLE OF CONTENTS

Foreword	1
Chapter 1	3
Chapter 2	17
Chapter 3	27
Chapter 4	43
Chapter 5	56
Chapter 6	70
Chapter 7	89
Chapter 8	109
Chapter 9	121
Chapter 10	132
About the Author	148

Foreword

For my mother, in whom I love to call the biggest "5ft 2" giant" of a woman I know; your bravery is unmatched, for not only living through that experience, but navigating through the trauma to share that life event with everyone around you. You are the personification of someone who has overcome by the blood of the lamb and the word of your testimony. I hope this book blesses people to be strong and brave in the time of adversity, just as you have been and that people, through your story can come to know the God who truly works miracles!

Sharnelle M. Mutembezi

How God Made a Way of Escape

"I cried for six months, not knowing what to do. I never thought in my wildest dreams this was going to happen to me".

1

IT WAS MAY 2011. And I was overcome with elation because I was on the verge of stepping out into a new adventure. At the time, I was working as the head administrator for a major fitness company. I was deeply rooted in the administrative affairs of the business and as an employee; one can say that I was content in my career at the moment. However, I weighed out the opportunity cost, quit my job and headed straight to Africa in hopes of doing business there. My husband, Dan, being the businessman that he is, took two weeks' vacation from his job as a consumer insolvency administrator in hopes of fulfilling an attractive potential that was proposed to him by his father and stepmother in Uganda. Fueled by ambition, Dan strongly believed that this opportunity was eventually going to provide a better life for him and his family. He hastily packed his bags, held us in his arms in a departing embrace and left throught the gates to catch his flight to Africa. I followed a week later, I went to Djibouti. We were supposed to meet in two days. Little did I know, this leisurely vacation would snowball into becoming quite the contrary!

Never heard of Djibouti? Djibouti is located on the horn of Africa. It is a country of dry shrub-lands with volcanic formations and Gulf of Aden beaches, yet desert. It is bordered by Ethiopia, Somalia and Eretria, which are predominantly Muslim countries, with the exception of Ethiopia. The common language is Somali, but the scholarly Djiboutians also speaks French as a result of the colonization by France in 1884. The climate of this region is dangerously hot with the temperatures reaching up tp 55 plus degrees Celsius at any point, which makes you wonder how people can live, let alone adapt to such unrelenting conditions. There is hardly any rain causing dry spells that last for months. Don't get me started on the sandstorms! They can occur at any given time of the day and terrotize the entire country with ominous howls of wind that entraps home and dust the land in it's reddish tinge. Uganda on the contrary, where Dan went, is located in eastern Africa and consist of diverse landscape from snowcapped mountains to great lakes, watefalls and wildlife. The official languages there are both English and Swahili. Swahili being a language that my husband was very well-versed in.

To the untrained eye, a business trip in such vast continent could seem daunting and cumbersome. But, when Dan asked me to join him in Africa, I accepted the invitation, since he insisted that my assistance was required. However, over the years, Dan had made countless commerce-focused trips to Africa before while ruiniting with his father during his downtime. I assumed that in our 20-plus years of marriage, if he was able to do it the number of times that he did, a two-week trip would be a walk in the park. What I did not take into consideration was the mere fact that I had not yet taken such an extensive trip abroad; just back and forth to Trinidad a couple times. Other than to visit the island, I had not really left North America in about nineteen years! I decided I wasn't going to let my travel inexperience to thwart out opportunity. However, the deciding factor was our three children. We have three children; two boys and one girl. At the time, our two oldest were away in University and our youngest son was still at home going into his senior year of high school. Knowing our two older child would come home in April for summer vacation, we planned on leaving during that time. We figured that we would be gone for two weeks, and our older children would take care of their younger brother. In our minds, this plan was practically foolproof!

    I had never heard of Djibouti before, yet I was shrouded in naïvete. I never felt the need to research the geographical cultural or political climate of this faraway land prior to my departure. All I knew was that Africa was normally hot and that I have to dress according to the temperature there.

Love has no barriers and it does not discriminate, love is the engine that fuels humans to do the impossible. Love is everything the bible describes it to be in 1 Corinthians 13. That's where the story begins between my husband and I. We met in Montreal, Canada during the late 80's coming from two different parts of the globe. Dan was born in Congo-Zaire, now known as the DRC. He and his family were forced to flee the country when he was about two years old due to the tragic political unrest happening at the time. He and his family lived in different countries in Africa. When he was 18 years old, he migrated to Canada and called it his home ever since.

I was born in the Caribbean, in the beautiful twin island of Trinidad and Tobago. My mother died when I was at the tender age of seven. As a result, I went to live with my grandparents on my father's side. Tradgedy struck once more when my grandmother suddenly passed away about four years later, and I was sent to live with my aunt, (my father's sister), who was also my godmother. With pain riddling my young life, I had the opportunity to migrate to Canada at the age of 24, and I took it. I was a young, single woman who wasn't looking for a relationship at the time. Be that as it may, Dan walked in to my life a few months after I arrived in Canada. He was charming, well dressed, and a gentleman, with the intelligence that would impress any scholar he came into contact with. He was French speaking, I was English speaking but as they say, there are no bounds, and we made it work despite the language barrier. We got married in the summer of 1990 and have been married for over 30 years. We have three wonderful children who are all in their mid and late twenties now. They are our rock; we love them to pieces. Throughput the years, we did our best to provide them with a sense of normalcy in an ever-changing world. We also made sure that they were solely devoted to Christ by enforcing Proverbs 22:6 which says "Train up a child in the way he should go, and when he is old, he will not depart from it".

Prior to leaving, I asked my sister Geena to keep an eye on our children. She was happy to provide this service as that was going to be a bonding time with her niece and nephews. Generously, she dropped everything and moved in to our home to be with our children, Dan and I felt more confident now that we knew they'd be left in good hands. This trip was also an opportunity to meet my father-in-law, Moses for the first time as he has because never visited Canada. Moses was always involved in politics in Africa. Which was why he never left even though his family lives all over the world. His mantra was always one of keeping balance and maintaining justice for his war striken home land of D.R Congo. Despite the fact he was currently living in Uganda. He lived a quiet life there with his wife, Jane. Jane use to to ask my father-in-law to call Dan almost every day. She would to speak to him and tell him about the wonderful opportunity she said was ready and waiting. Jane told him for him in Africa, in hopes of selling him the dream. She seemingly convinced Dan to finally go to Uganda to pursue the opportunity she said was ready and waiting. Jane told him she had everybody and everything in place, both the sellers and the merchandise lined up and waiting and they were ready to execute the plan. What is the plan, you may ask? The plan was simple: Go to Uganda, collect the gold, send the gold to Djibouti and in 2 days, meet the buyers. (Dan's role simply being that of a mediator). After hearing exactly how he would be involved, Dan spoke with his father to confirm what Jane was telling him was a safe endeavor. *He never thought he was walking into a trap all panned out by Jane because he trusted her, as she was his father's wife.* Dan told Jane again for the last time, "Make sure everything is ready by the time I arrive." She offered him full assurance as she had been made aware that many had sent broken promises.

    Jane told Dan they had 30 kilos of uncleaned gold, which was worth about two million US dollars at the time. She informed him that they were going to give him the gold to sell for them. Dan was into the precious stones business, and Jane kept assuring him allt sounded like a great opportunity for Dan to make some money because he was in to the precious stones business. We then contacted a family friend, cousin Irwin, a distant family member on my side of the family, whom I consider to be an uncle. He was the person to call when it came to that sort of business. He had been in the business for many years, and of course he would know buyers who could be interested in that amount of gold. Cousin Irwin's arrangement to meet with buyers was a bit long.

    The following Sunday we found ourselves in church as we usually do. Little did we know that there was a wolf in shepp's clothing sitting amongst us in our very own pews. As soon as we walked in, right there standing in the lobby was a was a mutual friend Jebu. He was a member of our church and an acquaintance of Dan. He too was African from the neighbouring neighboring country of Burundi; they both spoke French as they were a part of the small but expanding growing French community in our church. They started chatting, and one converstion led to another when he asked Dan how business was going. Dan began to explain what was going on with the Uganda situation. That he had been dealing with someone, but they were taking too long, and the people were pressuring him to act quickly. Right away Jebu ceased the opportunity and decided he would be able to help. Dan was elated that he could do something faster. In one week, Jebu had set up everything, He was and calling Dan back and forth for the planning. He mentioned to Dan that his best friend Mahmood, who is Djiboutian and living in Canada, knew people who would be interested in buying the gold. They had set up a flight for my husband and Jebu to go to Uganda in no time, to secure the merchandise. Meanwhile, Mahmood was also talking back and forth with the potential buyers in Djibouti. The agreement was settled. They concluded with an agreement that the seller would send the merchandise, gold to Djibouti, and they together would take it to Dubai to get it cleaned in order to get the maximum amount of money for it. They would then pay the sellers in Uganda for the unclean product, the way in which it was sent, they will sell the cleaned product and get the market price for it and split the profit amongst the four people respective, Dan, Ansar, jebu and Mahmood. It was going to be a lot of money. But soon after, it seemed as if God had jumped out the window and greed immediately crept in. We had no clue what was occurring on both sides and that we were walking into the middle of a trap. Both sides wanted to use us for their own greed. Dan and I decided he Dan, would go with the sellers in Uganda, and I would go with the buyers in Djibouti to prepare transaction that was supposedly about to occur. We were supposed to meet in two days in Djibouti to conclude the deal. We had spoken to cousin Irwin about our new arrangement with Jebu since we all attended the same church and they knew each other. Once the plan was finalized, cousin Irwin, who was a part of the church staff, spoke to the senior pastor about praying for Dan and I before heading off. He too knew about the deal and was also interested in working with us. And just before Dan, he called us into his office. There he prayed for us and blessed our journey as she along with everyone else felt that this was a big opportunity. When he was done praying, he turned toward me and said, "I don't know why you're going." I informed him that I was going to assist my husband. And with a look of uneasiness, she responded by saying" she understood.

It was time. Off Dan and Jebu headed for Uganda. I was to leave a week after for Djibouti. Dan's job was just simply to go to Uganda, collect the merchandise and send it to Djibouti. It was supposed to take two days to execute that task. And once completed, he was to join me in Djibouti, conclude the transaction, and upon completion, we would return to Uganda to meet and spend time with my father-in-law. Sounds simple right? When Dan arrived in Uganda his stepmother, Jane took him to meet with the suppliers. They brought him the box with the 30 kilos of gold to Dan, my husband inspected it to ensure that we were not getting ripped off by them with a magnetic piece of metal. He literally put his hands in it and felt it just to confirm that it was real. He concluded that it was, indeed pure refined gold. They even gave him a sample to send to the buyers in Djibouti. When the buyers received and tested the sample, they also confirmed that the gold was 98 percent pure.

Meanwhile, during the following few days, I packed my bags as Mahmood organized and booked the flight for him and me to travel together to Djibouti. I was excited, I had taken a lot of stuff including gifts for my father-in-law, medication in case we got sick and many of my fine clothes and jewelry on that trip. My children had been at home then for a few weeks, my sister went over to my house to stay with them. Everything seemed set for me and off I went on my new adventure. At the airport, my daughter asked me if I was crying because I was leaving them behind. I said no because I had nothing to worry about at that point in time. Also, I knew Dan was already in Africa, what could possibly go wrong? I was going to see him in a couple of days. It was an auspicious but lonf trip. We had a couple of layovers. Finally, we arrived in Djibouti. Ansar picked us up at the airport and took us directly to in a hotel he had reserved for us in downtown Djibouti. I did not get to see the city until the next day. The first thing I wanted to do was so talk to Dan. He was very happ that I had finally arrived When I asked him hoe he was doing, he said fine. Jebu too was happy that his best friend and partner in crime had arrived. Remember they hadn't met each other yet. After all they had planned and plotted this whole operation together. Dan remained in Uganda continuing the negotiations with the sellers.

    A couple days had gone by, but the shipment was not arriving in Djibouti for onr reason or the other. There was always an excuse for the delay. As the sellers never actually handed over merchandise to Dan. They told him that they would handle the courier themselves. when it came to the merchandise. Therefore, Dan had no control as to when the merchandise would arrive in Djibouti. I not at the time, but, one day after Mahmood had arrived, he had already started threatening and intimidating Dan. He told him, *"If we don't get the merchandise, we are going to keep your wife here in Djibouti; she is out guarantee"* Dan never told me that because he didn't want me to panic. After all, I was all by myself with people I did not really know. Never in my wildest dream had I ever fathom that they were capable of doing me harm. But Dan had taken their threat seriously. He immediately went and reported me kidnapped at the Canadian Embassy in Nairobi. It had become his worst nightmare; he never expected them to behave in such a manner. Afterall, we were supposed to be collaborating with each other because we had the same end goal in mind. They were getting more and more hostile. They were pressuring him to get the product over to them and Dan wanted nothing more than to do that, if only the people in Uganda would corporate.

What took place afterwards was just un-imaginable.

When greed and cunningness decided to show its ugly sides. Meanwhile, I had no clue what was going on behind the background. Back in Uganda - for Jane to come up with 30 kilos of gold, she had collaborated with a few people in order to come up with with the 30 kilos of gold. There were five people in total. Four men and she Jane had collaborated together to make up the group for the sum amount. But it seemed unusual for four males to collaborate with a woman, In Africa men and women don't usually work together in this kind of business because in that culture, women might seem inferior to men. But Jane was the main instigator. set up. She told them that she had a money chest in Canada, which was Dan, and used his own father, Moses, her husband to woo him to Africa so that they could con him. Not thinking that she was What a wicked person, the whole execution.

A week had gone by and nothing arrived in Djibouti. Suddenly, the sellers in Uganda demanded $30,000US from Dan. They claimed that they needed the money to provide the documentation for the origin of the gold. What's called "*The Certificate of Origin.*" You must have this documentation paper in order to move the gold out of the country or sell it. Ansar was the so called buyer, Dan informed him about the amount that was demamded and said it was as they said, essential in order to provide the papers. Ansar assured Dan that he was going to send the sum amount, as soon as possible, but instead of sending the money to Dan, Ansar decided to send the $30,000US with Mahmood and Jebu. After a couple of days, he flew them to Uganda to personally deliver the money to the sellers. We thought that was strange of Ansar for doing that. Why did he do it, did he not trust Dan enough to send him that mount of money? After all, he was previously sending money to him mostly on a daily basis mostly through Western Union to give to whomever was in charge of couriering the gold to Djibouti. They had been asking for money for about two weeks and more before but in smaller amount. Dan recalled as soon as the sellers received the $30,000US, they immediately shifted into another room and after about half an hour, they emerged with an envelope containing some documents. The documents looked real. They had the government stamp and all that was required for the document to be legitimate. But we then realized after all that, that the documents were made up yes, the **documents were fake**. Anyway the Ugandans departed without even saying goodbye. To Dan and the others. After that façade, Dan said he did not see any of them for a few days until Jane emerged and was acting really strange.

They had other plans. We later learned after all that charade; the sellers did not trust Ansar because he was Djiboutian. They concluded that, Djibouti was a poor country, and nobody in Djibouti would have been able to afford the purchase of 30 kilos of gold. But to me at the time, Ansar looked serious enough because he was getting more and more invested in the transaction process. The sellers thought they were probably thought they were scheming the Canadians. How sad. And they had no plans on sending the gold to Djibouti. Everything was a set up from the beginning. Jane and her cohorts were playing a dangerous game, to conspire against he buyers and still keep the gold. We believed that we were doing business with serious people, but little did we know, that people like to play games and to gamble with other people's lives and integrity.

2

JANE TOOK A BUS AND LEFT FOR CONGO. Before she left for Dr. Congo, she handed Dan a paper with a website written on it, and told him to just check the website so that he will be able to track the shipment. If he needs anything to just check the website for all the information pertaining to the arrival of the merchandise in Uganda, instead of calling her. There was a tracking number, an airline flight number for the cargo information that the gold was supposed to arrive in. Everything seemed to be there. The merchandise was scheduled to arrive in Djibouti via Ethiopian Airline on a certain date. Thhings lokked very optimistic. *But that information was false too.* How could they come up with such a detailed plan? Dan was the only person they had given that information to, and he decided to share it with Jebu, who was with him in Uganda at that particular time. He was there to pressure Dan to send the merchandise. Dan said,

Jehu went to the airport everyday to try to retrieve the merchandise before him. He did that without informing Dan he was doing so. Everybody was trying to outplay each other. How dishonest was he.

When the flight arrived, Jebu was right there, he tried to retrieve the merchandise but, they couldn't find the particular tracking number in their system. They instructed him to go back and check the website again to see if he had the right information. But nothing had changed. They informed him to go back and contact the sender to find out if they really sent the merchandise. Jebu had no other option but to go to see Dan, who was surprised that he (Jebu) had been going to check on the precious cargo behind his back. Dan thought they were working as a team. Nevertheless, the next day, they went together to Ethiopian airlines. They checked with the information they had again, they were both told the same thing. No such number and cargo exist for pickup. Then they relayed that somebody had already been to their office to check for the shipment and had threatened to sue them if the cargo did not arrive. How desperate and sad. The scheming was going on from both sides. The buyers thought they were going to out-smart Dan, but the sellers, but had already out-smarted everyone.

Two weeks had gone by and nothing was manifesting. Things were getting worse and worse for Dan. After that, Jebu tried to intimidate Dan. He had a brother-in-law who was serving as a general in the Ugandan army, He tried to set up a meeting between Dan and his brother-in-law to scare Dan with threats of putting him to jail. Anyway, Dan did not buy into Jebu's antics and for some reason, did not go to the meeting. Therefore, Jebu's plan failed. Dan was going through his own battle there in Uganda, but he did not tell me anything because he didn't want me to panic. He knew me very well. I was not a strong person, or should I say, I was a very fragile person by nature. Dan knew that if I had really what was really taking place, I would have been devastated and started panicking so he chose not to tell me. Which was a wise decision on his part. He was always protective of his family.

Now we were entering the third week, and time was of the essence. Dan's place of employment called the house and asked the children if he was back. They wanted to know when he was going to return home. When Dan called, they asked him, but he could not give them an answer because he himself did not know when he was going to get to go home. The company terminated his position after a month of absence and cited Dan for job abandonment. In the meantime, I had set everything up when it came to finances for the children to manage the day to day operations of the house. I had given my daughter my bank card for withdrawing money out of our bank account for whatever she needed to do. I emailed her from Djibouti explaining when different payments were going to draft out automatically from the account and when the other bills were due to be paid, but she still messed it up. It was her first time ever seeing or doing something like that, and she didn't quite know how to execute things. After a few months, everything ended up going south. What a nightmare that was for them

Dan decided to talk to his stepmother, Jane, who was then back in Uganda and explained to her what was going on that they never received the merchandise. He said he goy serious with her her and told her he wanted to talk to the person that was in charge of the whole thing. She said his name was John, and she would take him to meet with John the next day. When they went to John's house, Lo and behold, he was lying in a coma. Unable to even speak to them. Dan said he was puzzled. He kept on going to the hospital every day for a few days to see if the guy would wake up, but he was still in the coma. Dan said, John's family was very distraught. They were crying and praying for him to wake up. But of no avail. Dan felt compassion for them, and asked the family if he could pray for him, John. They said, "Yes," he went in the room, prayed for him, and left. Around 3:00 a.m. the nexy morning, Dan woke up to his phone ringing. It was John. He had awoken out of his coma and had called Dan to thank him for his prayers. *Dan remained persistent.* He wanted to get to the bottom of things. He spoke to John and asked him why the merchandise was never sent to Djibouti. He did not give him an answer.

A couple of days later, John asked if they could meet up in person. Both Dan and Moses, his father, went to the meeting. John once and for all decided that Dan was going too far by him wanting to know more about happened to the gold and why it wasn't sent to Djibouti, and when they were going to start acting on their promise? He was persistent because most importantly, he wanted our nightmare to be over so that he could finally het me out of Djibouti. Anyhow, John showed up at the meeting with two other people. As you may guess, one of them was was a General with his bodyguard. They were busy talking when John pulled Dan aside to speak with him privately. He said to him, they were instructed to get rid of him. But he couldn't go through with him because Dan was a good man. The bodyguard even saw the gun at the bodyguard's side. This was a different General. It wasn't Jebu's brother-in-law. The General implied that Dan was there to steal their gold, how absurd of them. They claimed that apparently, they had no clue what happened to the 30 kilos of gold in question. And was implying that Dan had stolen it. That's how deranged they were. Dan said they asked him to buy them some drinks, then Dan and Moses left. John saw Dan the next day and questioned him about Jane's whereabouts, since she was responsible for the arrangements. He himself did not know where to find her or what was going on with her. Dan told John he did not know of her whereabouts because he didn't want to end up playing their games. But then Dan learned that Jane had fled to Congo because somebody had attempted to kill her. I guess, if they spared Dan, she had to be the fall person because she was the one who brought Dan to them. Meanwhile my fathe-in-law had to clue about his young wife, Jane's involvement. He was only with the understanding that Jane had convinced him to bring his son to Uganda to conduct business. She took advantage of that poor old man. Moses used to ask Dan for money very often and in big amounts. He thought Moses needed the money to build a better life for himself, but there was only one problem. I am talking thousands of dollars that Dan would send. While Dan was in Uganda, he was able to find out that Jane had another family (a young family), living on the Congo border. Jane went back and forth to Condo. She used the money (sent by Dan) to build a house for her and her family there. Moses knew what she was in to, but he chose her. He was an old man with a young wife, so for him, he would have done anything to please her.

Meanwhile in Djibouti, Mahmood, Jebu, and I were staying at the same hotel in downtown Djibouti and would meet at a certain time every evening after Ansar was done working. One night, Mahmood called me over to his room. He saidtold he was going to see if he could get me an earlier flight back to Canada and demanded my return plane ticket. I wasn't aware of his plan. After a couple of days, I saw my ticket sitting on the table in his room but I genuinely thought he was trying to get me home early and didn't make anything out of it. I didn't think that he had planned not giving it back to me. However, as I mentioned before. I didn't really think anything of it. Also, one of my biggest problems was the food. I am already a picky eater, and the food in Djibouti was not good for me. Whenever I ate, I became sick to the stomach. I attempted to eat several times but was unsuccessful. Hence, Ansar had decided he would pick me up every day to take me to his house to eat lunch, they had their cook. His place was also very clean. They had everything going for them. They were renting a nice flat in a good area, where the tourists lived, and it was tastefully decorated. They also had people working for them. Luni, Ansar's wife, did absolutely nothing for herself. However, as they did not want their workers to understand what they were talking about, they modtly communicated with each other in French when they were at home except for when they were speaking directly to the worker, they spoke to them in Somali, that was the only language they understood. But everyone knew I was English so Luni and Ansar spoke English with me because they lived in Canada for some time, Ansar for 10 years and Luni for 18 years. They tried to make me feel comfortable whenever there. I presumed that it was good for me. But that did not last very long.

God knows all things. He is indeed the Omniscience God. I really do have a genuine love for children, Ansar and Luni had a six-month-old baby girl named Mika. On my first visit, Mika immediately drawn to me and we became good buddies through the time. It was my joy to go there every day just to see Mika, where I spent hours just playing and interacting with her. I came to learn, after a little while of being there, that because Mika was a dark-skinned baby, her mother, Luni, did not care so much for her. Instead, she had the babysitter and the maids take care of her. She did not show her a lot of affection; neither did she spend a lot of time with her baby. That was bizzare to me because I noticed that Mika expressed so much love and joy towards me. She was such a pleasure to be around. I used to sing to Mika. She loved to sing. I even thought her how to clap her hands, and she even started dancing when we were singing. She particularly loved the nursery song Old McDonald and If You happy and You know It. Mika would cry whenever anybody tried to pick her up, but not me, she ran to me. After a couple of months or so, because of Mika's development and character changed, she became very charming. The affection that she was expressing towards me, made Luni jealous. At one point in time Luni told Ansar that Mika didn't want to eat her food when I was present because she got too excited when she saw me, so he would ask me to leave the dining area when they were feeding her. That made me sad. Luni had finally gotten her way. Even my love for Mika brought her to jealousy, isn't that how it is supposed to be anyway? She got jealous for her own baby. That was not my intention, but it happened. God loves his little children and made it happen that way. ***I truly believed that my faith in God and baby Mika is what kept me going. Hence, they are the reasons I'm alive today.***

3

It was now three weeks into my stay at the hotel in downtown Djibouti. Ansar came to see me and told me that he was going to move me to his house until the deal was finalized. I said okay and called to inform Dan about the move to Ansar's, from which Dan already known. I guess Ansar had spoken to him before. Dan said he asked Ansar, "Are you kidnapping my wife because that's what it feels like." Ansar replied, "You can say that, but we will take good care of her." Dan never told me that for fear of me panicking.

Ansar came later that evening and moved me to his house. They had set up a room for me. I was okay with that because I was a bit lonely at the hotel too. More importantly, I was going to be with baby Mika and I did not know anybody else nor did I speak the language and couldn't go anywhere. It was also pretty quiet, which I liked. Djibouti is not a very big country, so things are not too far from each other. I learned that, in Africa, the rich are very rich and the poor is very poor. The people with money live in certain gated areas, where their houses are barred around by concrete and barbed wire.

The guardian's belongings were always outside; they were not allowed in the house unless they were invited. They used an empty lot as their toilet, and they had to bathe outside in the back of the house. They kept their own utensils outside with them and would take their dishes to the kitchen window to pick up their meals. These individuals would watch the house day and night, and they also ran errands for their masters. Luni had two guards that she would call on them anytime of the day to run errands for her. One of them was very loyal to doing whatever she asked.

Meanwhile, when I was exiting the hotel, Ansar stopped at the front desk to pick up my passport. When you're staying in a hotel in Africa, you have to leave your passport at the front desk. I thought he was doing me a favor by picking up my passport. Little did I know, he was confiscating it, that he couldn't wait to get a hold of it to put it in his volt with the rest of the ones he was holding. Then I would not be able to leave. I did not realize he never gave it back to me, and I didn't ask him for it either. At one point, Ansar introduced me to people who were working for them, some for 6 years, others 10, some longer, but they were never allowed to leave Djibouti to see their families in those many years because they had confiscated their passports and were holding them. These people seemed happy to work for them. They were hard workers, but from what I observed, they may or may not have been aware they were being held against their own wills. For that reason, I had never made anything out of it when Ansar introduced me to them and told me the number of years they were in Djibouti working for them. They couldn't have left anyway. Ansar and his family seemed so genuine at the beginning, but it was only a façade.

In the meantime, during all that transition, Jebu left Djibouti and returned to his job in Canada while Mahmood remained in Djibouti. After a few days, when Ansar came home from work he asked me to get dressed becauseone he wanted to show me something. He drove me to the airport and showed me Mahmood leaving to board a plane back to Canada. He said to me, "You see the guy walking next to him, he is a plain clothes police officer. Mahmood is a bad guy, and he and Jebu will not be bothering you and your husband, Dan, anymore."

Ansar was trying to make us feel we could trust him. He had taken over the operation. He had now decided that he and his brother-in-law was going to handle everything. They had gotten rid of the loose ends, Mahmood and Jebu, and were going to tag team together and deal with it the way they knew how. Like they had been holding the others. After all, they had me right where they wanted me. He said to himself, *I've got the biggest bait in my hands, and now I will be able manipulate Dan into finishing the deal* as he would often say. He realized by then what Dan's secret was, his love for family. It was not going to be easy for him though because he was holding the wrong person. Both Jebu and Mahmood were temporarily out of the picture since they were back in Canada, and Ansar warned them not to speak to Dan about the business again once they had arrived home. He was going to be handling things himself in his own way. But as I said before, I did not know what I had gotten myself caught up in. Ansar and his brother-in-law were the mafia of Djibouti, and they were experts in kidnapping people. But they had kidnapped the wrong person this time. Because as Psalm 105:15 says *"Do not touch my anointed ones; do my prophets no harm."* **They had their way with me for some time, but when God was ready to have his way, no one, I mean no one or nothing could stop Him.**

My devastation:

It was the middle of June, a month had passed, and our youngest son's soccer team was hosting a visiting team from South America. Dan and I had promised to put up some of the boys in our home. The team was to arrive on June 25th. As the time was approaching, I went to Luni while she was giving Mika a bath.

I said, "I am going home now because I was supposed to put up some visiting boys for my son's soccer team in our home." **Luni replied, "You can say that we kidnapped you because you are not going home."** Ansar was standing next to her, but he didn't say anything. When she said that, my heart sunked into my chest. I said to her, "But I have to go home to my children." Suddenly, the thought hit me, *I am really kidnapped*. I said to them, "Guys, you are holding the wrong person. I am not strong physically or emotionally." *Luni said, "Well, you're not going home until I get back my 30,000 dollars."* That was news to me. It was the same amount they sent Jebu and Mahmood to personally take to the sellers. I was clueless as to what she was babbling about because I really was unaware of this 30,000USD! *What's happening here?* I thought to myself.

I was completely caught off-guard, realizing what was really happening to me. I was so naïve in trusting these people and did not for a minute think that I was kidnapped! When realization hit, I began sobbing uncontrollably. I thought to myself, I was far from home, and I knew no one there. How was I going to get out? What about my children, my husband, My home? I just wanted to go home. I was becoming so overwhelmed by my dilemma. Ansar, Mahmood and Jebu had planned my kidnap since day one of my arrival to Djibouti and I had no clue!

I couldn't stop crying. Ansar said to me, "All the time you weren't crying why are you crying now? You're being treated well." The atmosphere in the house suddenly changed. I called my husband, who was still in Uganda at the time and told him about what had just transpired between Ansar, Luni, and I. He asked me to pass the phone to Ansar. He pleaded with him to send me home, but Ansar refused. Dan told him I needed to go home to take care of the children. Ansar responded, "Your children are big, I'm not sending her home." Dan felt hopeless because he already knew what was happening. Dan asked to talked to me again and calmed me down. He told me to just stay and wait until the deal was done. That was how I stopped crying. My husband realized his hands were tied. He was upset at himself and sad, knowing I had just found out that I was being taken hostage. He then tried for a couple of weeks to bring the deal to fruition but nothing seemed to be working. After trying for a couple more weeks, he decided to leave Uganda to return home to Canada and work side by side with the Canadian government to get me home. Both he and his father, were sending emails and making phone calls around the clock to ensure I made it home and in one piece.

Dan had already filed a complaint with the Canadian embassy in Nairobi Kenya, when Mahmood had made the first threat of kidnapping me on the very first day I arrived in Djibouti so the Canadian government was already aware of my current situation. When the Canadian government finally contacted Dan, they explained to him that they were not like the Americans who would personally intervene in the negotiations for their citizens who are in trouble abroad, but they would get me overseas Canadian Consular help. That they had already contacted their Canadian Consulate office there in Djibouti to inform them about my situation. Meanwhile I had no clue what was going on in the backgroud, but a few days later, Dan called me and told me he was leaving Uganda to go back home to Canada. I was devastated. I began to feel abandoned. I started sobbing breathlessly even though Dan was in Uganda and I was in Djibouti, I still felt close to him because we we at least on the same continent. I felt as though my heart was ripping out of my chest again. Things were getting more and more graver for me and I didn't know what to do. It was a bigger nightmare for me. I didn't know what to do. I didn't quite understand at that moment but after I understood Dan also had to look out for his own safety. He said he didn't tell anyone, not even our own children nor the people in Uganda, including his father that he was leaving. He just packed his bags, took a taxi, went straight to the airport, boarded the plane and headed to Canada.

    I was now all alone in Africa and did not know what to do lacking knowledge of culture and language. I was halfway around the world all by myself. I had learnt

French but never spoken it on a daily basis. For this reason, I was not very comfortable at conversing in French and only spoke English with my captureres. I did tell them I understood French but they did not take me seriously. Especially Luni, she thought I was dumb because whenever they tried to interrogate me about the deal, I kept saying I didn't know. But I really didn't know anything. Dan never wanted to make me worried so he kept all the troblous details from me.

With that in mind, Ansar and Luni, mostly spoke French in the home because they did not want their workers to know what they were talking about, as the workers did not speak nor understand French. They were poor and uneducated people that drift around from country to country in Africa to find work for their survival and to send money for their families. They were from neighbouring Somali speaking countries and did the work that was undesirable to the general Djiboutian population, but in reality, they are working as slaves to people like Ansar and his family.

Meanwhile, When Dan arrived home, he rang the doorbell, my sister Geena answered. She said, when she opened the door. She was surprised and confused, she did not recognize Dan. He had become darker and looked thinner than normal, his whole demeanor had changed. Only when he spoke, she realized it was him. Dan was very stressed with everything that was going on. It was really affecting him, so much that it took a toll on his health. He also said that he believed he and his father were poisoned sometime during his time in Uganda, and at one point they became very sick and ended up in the hospital.

Finally, our children had at least one parent at home with them, how wonderful. My sister Geena was then able to leave and go to her own house to take care of her affairs. But it wasn't the same with mom not being there. Even though I was in Africa, I was still mothering them. My daughter had hurt her shoulder. She fell down and broke her shoulder in front of her apartment when she was going to school in Ottawa and could not use her left hand because she was in constant pain. Sometimes she would just be lying down and her shoulder would just pop out of place. I felt sorry for her. I used to pray for her and tell her what to do.

By that time, all the rest of my family had found out what had happened to me. The rest of my sisters and my brother were devastated. They thought they were never going to see me again. They said to themselves that I was left in Africa to die., which was literally true, *but God had other plans*. The next day my brother Joe went over to our house. He wanted personally to hear from Dan where I was and what had happened his sister; he was very upset. However, he said, when he saw Dan's face, he was filled with compassion seeing how grief stricken he appeared.

He knew Dan always travelled for business, but he did not know that this time I had gone with him to Africa. Dan told him exactly why I went and what had transpired. Furious, he asked Dan again, "But why did you take my sister to Africa?" He told Dan, "You better do everything in your power to bring my sister back home."

Joe then decided it was time for him to intervene. He asked Dan to call Ansar so he could speak to him and find out what had to be done to get me home. I was very happy to hear Joe's voice. Anyway, when he spoke to Ansar and asked him why he was holding his sister. Ansar told him he would send me home but they would have to make a swap, *to send Dan over to Djibouti then he would let me go*. After they were done talking, Ansar said, "I like your brother Joe. The next day, Joe went over to our house again, he wanted to speak to Mahmood and Jebu. He said when he spoke to Mahmood, they tried to be pleasant with each. He concluded, Mahmood was an interesting guy. During the conversation, he tried to get him to trust in him. By doing so, Joe found out some more information about Mahmood. Like his location in Canada and more about his family. We did know a little bit about him, but did not have a lot of details on him because everything happened so fast.

Joe was now in the thick of things. Now he had established himself with my kidnappers; he had spoken to everyone in the midst of the mess except for Jehu. Jebu pretended to be neutral. Joe even spoke to my pastor at the time and cousin Irwin. I clearly remembered Ansar saying that Jebu had instructed he put me in jail. Although Jebu and Mahmood were now in Canada and did not have any contact with Ansar, they were still pressuring and threatening Dan. Mahmood confided in Joe and told him that Dan was a liar that he had tricked them. That was the reason why they were holding me. Meanwhile, Joe said he had friended Mahmood enough to find out more about his family and exactly where he lived. He said, if it had come down to showing up at Mahmood's house as a last resort, he would have done that.

Mahmood and Jebu tried to convince Joe to get Dan to fly over Djibouti without him realizing it. They said, they were going make a swap, Dan's life for mine; for Dan to really buy into believing that they were going to let me go. Dan knew they would have held both of us and threw him in jail there in Djibouti with their vigilante justice. Dan wasn't a dummy; he had been in Africa a few times and knew how they operated. But frankly, he would have done anything just to get me back home. And if it had come to that, he would have willingly done whatever he had to do.

Greed and the length people would go to for money.

While all of this was happening, Ansar got a call from the Canadian Consulate in Djibouti. He told him, "The Canadian government is saying that you kidnapped a

Canadian here in Djibouti, where is the person?" When Ansar was done talking to him, Ansar's face changed, he looked very angry. He asked, "Is it true that your husband said we kidnapped you?" Remember, my husband did not tell me that he had filed a complaint at the Canadian embassy in Nairobi Kenya because he didn't want me to panic. Ansar was so furious, I got scared. Trembling, I said to him, "No I was not kidnapped." Then, he started coercing me to say that I was there in Djibouti because I wanted to be there. "You wanted to come, right?" he asked. I replied, "Yes," as I was fearing for my life. Also, they were the only people that I knew in Djibouti. I was in the other side of the world all by myself, I had to be cautious. What was I supposed to do next? He then told me to pack up my suitcase, that he was going to take me to the Canadian Consulate's office. I was scared, but hearing I was going to see the Canadian Consulate made me believe I was going to get to go home. That same evening, we went to the Consulate's office. Upon arrival, there waiting outside was Ansar's brother-in-law, Omar.

Dr. George, the Consulate General, who was also a medical doctor and runs his own medical clinic out of the same office ther in Djibouti. He runs one of the biggest medical clinics there. We had to sit and wait a little to see him. He eventually ccame and called us in to his office. The first thing he did was ask Ansar for my passport, already knowing he was in possession of it. Ansar pulled my passport out of his shirt pocket, placed it partly on the desk, not letting go of it and immediately picked my passport up and put it directly back into his pocket. Dr. George then said to me in front of Ansar and his brother-in-law, "If this is a criminal matter, you will need a lawyer."

Omar then left the office and went outside to wait for us. Meanwhile, Ansar and Dr. George began to discuss about me getting a lawyer. Dr. George gave me a list of names and phone numbers of female lawyers. I didn't know anything about lawyers in Djibouti, I looked confused. He then contacted a lawyer, but I did not retain her. He and Ansar was discussing back and forth. After that, Ansar picked up my suitcase and we left. As we were leaving, Omar said to Dr. George, "Bon voyage," meaning have a good trip. I was confused. I thought Dr. George was going away, but the next day, he saw me again. Then, days later, he was still there.

Confused, I was trying to make sense of everything that happened that night. Ansar took me back to right his house and told me they were going to put me in jail, I needed to call my husband and let him know. When I called, Dan tried to explain to Ansar, that I had nothing to do with their disagreement. Therefore, he should not put me in jail. Ansar was very furious because he finally got caught and was deemed a kidnapper. He did not want to hear anything. He hung up the phone and told me to go and get some rest because we were going to the courthouse first thing in the morning. I had taken a copy of the business corporation papers with me in order to open an account for the transferring of the payment of transaction that would have taken place there in Djibouti. You just can't take large sums of money out of a country and send to another country. There is a process to go through. Anyway, I didn't know when they had gone through my suitcase and took the papers out. I guess Luni had taken it while we were at the Consulate's office. They somehow wanted to prove I was a part of the business, that I was also to be held resposible. It was obvious they were trying to find a way to link and persecute me.

    I did not get a lot of sleep that night. As soon as morning arrived, Ansar told me to get ready were going to the courthouse. I was scared out of my wits, I was thinking, *I don't know what is going to happen to me next.* My husband and I did not take any money from these people neither did we try to scam anyone. We just got caught up in their schemes and I was the one paying the price for it. There was no transaction between any party, and unfortunately, Dan and I were the ones caught up in the middle of the others web of lies and deceit. We were going through similar loss as they were because we had forsaken everything in order go there for business, and we had the most to lose. Everyone knew that.

    When we arrived at the courthouse, Luni also

accompanied Ansar. She went as the interpreter. When we arrived, I was asked to sit down on a chair. A gentleman approached. I was unsure as to whom he was. If he could have been judge or lawyer. He looked at me and began speaking to me directly in Somali; then Luni started interpreting. Then Ansar pulled out the corporation papers. I was stunned when I saw him with them in his hands because I never gave it to them. He said to the gentleman, "You see she is also responsible because she is a part of the business." Then he looked up at Luni and asked, "Who is this interpreting for her?" Ansar said, "My wife." The gentleman shook his head in dismay. He then looked at me and shook his head. Speaking in French he replied, "Look at her. If you put her in jail, she is going to die." I looked frail and frightened, and he was aware of that. I had lost a lot of weight even though I was already a small person. He decided there and then, there was no way that he was going to send me to jail (my first angel).

They left the courthouse very disappointed with that decision. Luni said to me, "You are very lucky." Nonetheless, they had planned out for the outcome. They had the sheriff waiting outside to transport me to the police station where Ansar had already filed a complaint against me. Ansar then escorted me straight to the sheriff's car. Even though he did not get what he was hoping for. I got in the Sherrif's car, what I was told to do? I was only following his orders as he was trying to bring the full law against me. Anyway, Ansar followed us to the police station. Ansar walked in and signed this big book. I had no clue what was taking place. There was a young police officer in attendance, thin and tall. When Ansar was done and left, the young man opened the book, read Ansar's complaint filed against me and the amount claimed, then looked up at me and said, "Wow, this is a lot of money, you're going to take a long time to pay this. Don't worry. Everything will be okay." Then, they escorted me into this room with a cot in it and told me I could get some rest. I did not understand. All I knew was that I was in jail.

    Scared and shaking, I did not know whatwas going to happen to me next, or how long I had to stay there. The place was in very poor condition. It was difficult to tell the difference, whether it was a jail cell or not. Before I went into the room, I asked if I could call Dr. George, the Canadian Consulate. They called him for me, but I could not reach him. They then escorted me into the room. I just sat there observing everything that was going on around me. People kept going in and out, bringing criminals in. They stripped the men stripped them and put them in a place located at the back of the station that was barred around that looked like a coupe. Afterwards, I realized they were being placed into custody there. Whether I was in a real jail cell or not at the time, all I knew was that I was in jail. Aparently Dr, George was aware of everything that was happening.

A couple hours later, another young man walked into the police station. He was in plain clothes and sat on the outside of the room that I was in. He began speaking to me in English. Everybody around had heard about me. He said, "Don't worry. Everything will be alright." He also shared he was a police officer, and he came in to sleep. Most of the officers wear plain traditional clothes, which is part of their culture. I waited and waited. It was terrifying, and I was exhausted. Around 2:00-3:00 p.m., Ansar walked into the police station and brought me a sandwich and a drink. Of course, I couldn't eat. After all, I was thinking, *you threw me in jail and then tried bringt me food to eat? The nerve...* I pushed the food aside and just sat there. Around 5:30 p.m., Ansar returned to the police station. Believe it or not, I was happy to see him. Ansar signed the big book, and I was released. He took me back to their home. I was speechless. Luni said again, "You're lucky, some people don't have anybody to bring them food while in jail. She went on to explain to me that I wasn't really in a jail cell. I was utterly confused. What did I know? The condition of that the place looked and felt like jail to me. What an emotional roller coaster I was in.

4

THE NEXT DAY MY LIVING arrangements suddenly changed. Ansar established new rules. There would be no more air conditioning for me, which was one of the worst things they could have ever done to me. As I mentioned before, the temperature would always be over 40 degrees Celsius every single to a whopping 55+ degrees Celsius. It was extremely hot. I would have to sit in one place under a ceiling fan and not move in order to get a break from the heat. I used to put a chair outside in the evening when the sun went down and just sat there while reading my Bible, staring at the concrete fence for hours just praying and crying. I never blamed God for anything. I always asked myself why did I go to Djibouti? Most nights, I would sit out there until 3:00 a.min the morning., because I could not sleep. I had to force myself to sleep. It was difficult to eat; therefore, I would put a piece of bread in my mouth and then drink something in order to swallow it. The food couldn't go down.

I had lost so much weight, my clothes could no longer fit me. There was a wardrobe in the room that I slept in, filled with Luni's clothes that she didn't wear. I went through it and found a couple of her loose dresses. She had given me permission to wear them. I would wear one and wash the other. That was my routine. Also, because of the heat, I had developed a terrible heat rash around my shoulders and neck that just kept getting messier and messier. That was a big problem for me. One of many.

Nonetheless, remember cousin Irwin, he would be the key person in talking and negotiating Ansar. He was my second angel who assured me I could call on him anytime. When things got out of control, I would call him, and he would plead with Ansar not to carry out the threats that he had planned towards me at the time.

I was not allowed to leave the house unless Ansar or Luni took me out, and that was only to visit their family or to go the grocery store or to do something with them. Ansar drove directly in and out of the garage. The guardians would open and close the gate exiting or returning. We left mostly in the evening or at night too. They hardly did anything during the day. Both their families did not mind me hanging around because I looked like them. They even at one point in time tried to get me to wear their traditional clothes. I told them I did not know if my husband would like that. Luni tried to accuse me many times of petty little things, but Ansar always scolded her. He realized that I was not a troublemaker and carried myself in a certain manner, so he always defended me. I quickly came to the conclusion that Luni was a bit jealous of me. She'd try to find anything to disqualify me, but to no avail. I believe the jealously stimmed from Muslim men being allowed to have several wives, she probably felt insecure. But however, only one thing consumed my thoughts, getting home to my family, nothing else phased me.

Luni and Ansar were between 31-33 years old. I am sure they were not aware of my age, probably because I looked younger, but I was 46yrs old at the time. I am generally petite person. Anyway, whatever her reason was, I didn't care, and I was not concern about them and their lives.

After a few months, to keep things going in the house. Our older son had secured a summer job during his break from university and after a few months, he started contributing towards household expenses. My daughter. also started working and contributed towards the house as well. I tell you nothing moves or motivates us more than being a close-knit family who works together. That always pulled us through. We could have loss everything.

Hence, when Dan arrived home, he was able to focus on continuing to work on my case with all parties including the Canadian government. He was still trying his best to get the product delivered in order to get me home. He explored many options, but continued having road blocks. He was devastated and helpless. We had been through several unforeseen circumstances, but none prepared us for the distress the family was experiencing.

Meanwhile the so-called person who was in charge of couriering the merchandise to Uganda that was demanding, money mostly on a daily basis; he said to send the gold to Djibouti when Dan was there, contacted him a couple weeks after he arrived in Canada. He tried to convince him to pay him $20,000US, and promised that they would finally send the merchandise to Djibouti. But Dan did not buy in to his antics. Dan knew then what they were about. The damage had already been done and with grave casualty. Dan hired a lawyer out in Uganda to search for the location of the address of shipment company that they claimed they were using to presumably courier the merchandise to Djibouti. After the investigation, the lawyer concluded that there was no such address in Uganda, Even the office was address was made up. When Dan refused to send the $20,000US to them, they resorted back to Mahmood and Jebu, who still sent them money ranging from 2,000 to 7,000USD. But still, nothing was sent, I am not sure when it stopped.

Anyhow, Ansar and his friends came up with the conclusion that somebody had to pay the price for their greed and that was going to be Dan and his family. Dan and the children were very distraught. And to include no one in Uganda was aware of my kidnapping in Djibouti. Dan was specifically warned not to tell anyone that I was being held against my will. Nevertheless, Dan told his father, Moses. Moses became very worried and started planning with Dan on how to rescue me from his side there in Uganda. He suggested that I should get an African passport and when I do, they would send somebody in to sneak me out of Djibouti.

It was now the beginning of July and Ramadan had begun. The night before Ramadan Ansar said to me, "You cannot read your Bible anymore. You have to read the Quran."

I replied, "I was born into the church, and I will always remain a Christian." Luni was right there. She laughed and said, "Don't worry with Ansar." He is just joking. But he was serious.

They tried their best to convert me to Islam. During Ramadan, Luni would come in front of me wherever I was sitting inside and spread her mat to pray. I just looked at her, smiled, and walked away. They knew I was a Christian and often saw me quietly reading my Bible. I would pray silently. They never really heard me or physically saw me praying, but they knew I was. Luni used to show me some online teaching by a gentleman from India who claimed he was a Christian, but he had converted to Islam. She did this everyday for two weeks. I politely looked and listened to his teachings and discussions. He quoted scripture verses, especially from the New Testament. He knew them by heart. One day while listening to him, I totally lost it when I heard him say he believed the Bible, but God had no children! How could Jesus claim to be the Son of God? He vehemently denied Jesus! I told Luni I could not listen to him anymore, and I could never convert to Islam because that man did not believe whom Jesus claimed to be, the Son of God; even though he professed to know the scriptures. She then left me alone. Also, around that time, one of her sisters came over to the house to participate in the Ramadan rituals. She asked me if I was going to fast with them. I said no; then she said to me, "Where is your solidarity?" I just laughed. I said to myself, I don't have to tell her or show them when or if I am fasting. But I did fast for one week unto my God, the Lord Jesus Christ. I was immediately reminded of the scripture verse in Mathew 6:5, "And when you pray, do not be like the hypocrites. For they love to pray standing in the synagogues and on the street corners to be seen by men. Truly I tell you, they already have their reward."

    As Muslims, everybody in the house, including the workers, were supposed to be fasting and praying right? But when Luni and Ansar went out, the workers cooked and ate amongst themselves and hurriedly washed the pots and dishes and put them in their respective places before they returned. They acted as though nothing happened and appeared hungry as if they were fasting whit the rest of the household. Luni was a very cruel task master to her workers. She created difficult work for them during the Ramadan time and worked them harder. When they were hungry and weak, she made them work in the extreme heat; washing and cleaning the windows; and scrubbing the patio. She would find all sorts of odds and ends, tasks to be completed in and outside the house. she also sent them to run errands all day in that heat.

    Suddenly I noticed that Luni began to act very strange a few days into the fast. She would leave the room whenever Ansar entered, slamming the doors shut. When she went into the bedroom, she would lock the door so he couldn't get in. They would normally eat together, but this time she refused to eat with him. It got so bad between the both of them that Ansar's mother had to intervene. She and Ansar's sister went to the house and met with Ansar in the family room for a few hours. Later on that night, everything seemed good between Luni and Ansar again. Not only was it good, but they couldn't keep their hands off each other for a few days. I was able to find out their problem. He had promised he would send me home before Ramadan started, but he didn't and I guess my presence was disturbing their peace. Anyway, that was the reason why she was behaving in such a manner. She felt like he had tricked her. So, he promised her again, as soon as Ramadan was done, he was going to send me home.

Meanwhile, the next night when I fell asleep, I had a dream. It was the first of three very vivid dreams during that time in captivity in Djibouti. I dreamt of my aunt, Angel, who I grew up with, but she had brrn dead for a few years. That had never happened before. It was a very eerie feeling. I dreamt that we were in a room that looked like the one in which I slept in. She was sitting at a table and she said to me, "They were going to build a room for you next to my room, but I begged them not to, and they built a balcony instead for you." After hearing those words, I immediately left the room and went out on the balcony where I saw green grass for miles and miles away beyond my eyes could see. I then awoke from my sleep, terrified, thinking why did I dream about my aunt, Angel? It was really bothering me, but I tried not to think about it. I said to myself, I will soon forget about it. But when I called my family, Dan immediately asked me, "What did you dream? I asked him why? He asked again. I said no. I didn't want to talk about it, but he insisted and wouldn't let it go. I then told him a bit of the dream, we did not make anything of it. I did not talk about it anymore nor did Dan ask again because it just didn't make sense to us at the time. I was creeped out after dreaming my dead aunt Angel.

Things were now better between Ansar and Luni. When suddenly, baby Mika, their daughter, became very sick. Luni sensed something was happening. She got very angry again with Ansar and said to him, "I told you to send her home." She believed my presence was the reason why baby Mika got so sick. She knew there was a spiritual battle going on in her home. But I knew that that battle was not against flesh and blood. A few days later, Ansar also fell ill and that was when she lost it. She pleaded again with Ansar to send me home. He agreed again and promised he was going to take me home himself this time, when Ramadan was over. He also told to me, that he himself was going to take me home to my husband. Anyway, he and baby Mika went to see the doctor and was better after a few days.

During that time, Dr. George, the Canadian consulate, called the house and asked me how I was doing. He told Ansar that he wanted to see me for an update. I was very frail and weak. He then asked me if I was sleeping. I said no, and I just wanted to go home. I knew he was the only one that could help me to do that but I was unaware at the time that he was working with my capturers. He answered, "Tell your husband to get the people their money." He was familiar my story. He then prescribed me medication to put me to sleep and some other blood building medication. One of the medications was MAG3. I had never heard of it before, but I presumed he was a doctor and he was giving me medication that was for my best interest. The iron pills that he prescribed me, were for pregnant women. I later learned MAG3 is a compound chelated medication with the radioactive element – technetium-99. Anyway, I was not feeling any better. Time after time, Ansar would always ask me if I was taking my medication. I always said, "Yes." But the medication wasn't helping me, I kept feeling worse. I guessed he wanted me to stay alive. I slept a little more because that was what the MAG3 was meant to do. But my situation was so bad, I was deteriorating more and more.

However, after when it about 5 months or so into my captivity, I realized that Dr George was sending fake reports to the Canadian government. He was repoting that I was doing well even though he wasn't seeing me very often. He sent many reports to the Canadian government without seeing me. They kept telling my family that they had heard from Dr. George and that I was doing well. However, the Canadian government knew that my situation was grave and were very concerned about my well-being. They called my family every day to make sure that they were in contact with me. They assured them that they were doing everything to get me back home to them in Canada.

In the meantime, Ramadan was over, and remember Ansar said he was going to take me home, personally? Apparently, he had already purchased the first-class tickets for us to leave as soon as Ramadan was done. When that day arrived, Ansar decided to stay home. He locked himself in the bedroom, closed the curtains and slept all day. When Luni got home and saw me him in the house, she was furious. They bagan to argue. It was so bad, I heard them through the window. Unknowing to me, I did not know that I was supposed to go home on that day. But like Pharoah, he had changed his mind again.

With all the stress I was going through, I was bleeding for about three weeks. I decided to tell Luni, who then told Ansar. He made another appointment for me to see Dr. George. But this time, he had sent his brother-in-law Omar, to take me to the appointment. Omar pretended ro be very friendly. He told me I should visit their house sometime. Whenever I wanted to go just let him know, and he would pick me up.

When Dr. George saw me, he decided to prescribe me more medication that would sedate me. He prescribed me a liquid medication in little vials. It was very costly and needed to be refrigerated. Ansar did not mind paying for it. My family could not send me any money or anything because Ansar and his cohorts were supposedly in full control over me. I don't remember the name of the medication, but as I took it, a couple seconds after, I couldn't even wal. I literally bumping into the walls. I couldn't keep my eyes open or my head up. I had big blue spots all over my body. Meanwhile, Ansar being certain that if I took my medication. It didn't matter that he was destroying me and my family by holding me against my will. I said, "Yes," but I had lessened down the dosage and eventually stopped taking it.

It was getting harder and harder for me to go on. I felt like the walking dead. That gave Luni a better excuse for me not to interact with baby Mika. She asked me not to pick her up or play with her anymore. I getting weaker and weaker. My life was just dimishing from me and I was just devastated.

Around that time, I had a second dream about my aunt, Angel again. I dreamt that Luni was gardening. My Aunt Angel was watching her. She asked Luni, "When are you going to send her home?" Luni did not respond. A gentleman that was sitting on a bench facing the fence said in a loud voice "Tomorrow." I did not see his face, just his back. This time, I was not scared of the dream. The next day, I woke up feeling very optimistic, thinking this is the day, I was finally going to go home. But at some point during the day, I was looking through a long mirror in the hallway. Suddenly, I looked up and saw a Luni looking at me with such great contempt! I was taken aback. I couldn't understand why the hostility. However, the day went by, evening came and nothing happened, nobody said anything to me. I was disappointed andcrushed. As I had called my family and told them that I was finally coming home. When the evening came, I went to the back watched the planes fly by over my head.

5

As September arrived, I started to grow very weary. It was now three and a half months since I had touched Caadian soil. At that time, whenever I closed my eyes, I would just see those brick holes that were on top of the concrete fence in front of the house. I thought I was going to go crazy. Time was of the essence. Every day felt worse and worse for me. My children had to go back to school. My two oldest children were supposed to go back to the University of Ottawa, which is about a 4 1/2 hours, drive away from where we lived. and my youngest son was beginning grade 12, the most critical year for high school students. The older children decided not to return back to Ottawa. Eventually my older son thought he would try to return but could not continue because he could not focus. They both had summer jobs and continued working and taking care of their younger brother who turned seventeen that August. All three of my children attended the same elementary and high school, but my youngest decided after three weeks into grade 12, that he was going to switch to another school that was more recognized for its athletics. I begged him not to, but he had made up his mind that that was what he wanted to do. I finally said, "Okay, if you want to. Go ahead and make sure you pass school and get your high school diploma" (By-the-way he did and is now in his last year of University).

    Unexpectedly, Luni decided that she did not want me to use the laptop anymore and complained to Ansar that I broke it and needed to be fixed. That was the only way for me to get to communicate with my family. The problem was they were getting tired of not finding the information they were looking for. The next day Ansar brought somebody home to check the laptop, and the guy decided that he would take it with him for a few days in order to repair it. During those few days, I was very worried, I could not contact my family and I knew they were worried about me. When they brought the laptop back home, there was no sound. They had tampered with the volume on the laptop. We saw each other only and had to start typing our conversations. Soon after that, when Ansar came home in the evening, every day, he would take the laptop and go into the family roo. He, spent hours reading our conversation from the night before and throughout that day. We had spoken a lot to each other, especially during the night because of the time difference.

Also, I could not sleep because I had no peace of mind. I was confused and restless.

One day Ansar was going to work in the afternoon. I was talking to Dan on the laptop, and he asked me if he could use the laptop because he wanted to check something quickly. As you remembered, we could not talk to each other, and instead we typed our conversations. I motined bye to Dan because Ansar wanted to grab the laptop. I tried to cut off our communication quickly. Dan could see him too. In my swiftness, I pressed the wrong button. Whatever I touched, and lo and behold, it went straight to our conversation that we had just typed. I was shocked. I quickly glanced at the messages but pretended I didn't say anything. Then I cut Dan off and Ansar took the laptop. Right away it dawned on me what was going on. He was reading our conversations while locked in the family room for all those hours. When I eventually called Dan again, I told him what I saw, and we decided that we were going to talk in to talk in codes especially when we were referring to Ansar. Evwn though when we spoke about them, it was nothing that we did wrong or right but about their behavior toward us. Ansar could have recorded and read as much as he wanted, but he did and could not find anything. Dan I had nothing to hide anfd our conversations were mainly about my well-being and the children.

However, at some point, we had decided to call

Ansar Pharaoh. And that was because he kept changing his mind about sending me home. He had no clue we were referencing to him when he read the name Pharaoh. There were a lot of strange things happening. Luni thought these things were happening in her house because I was there. But as I said, they were the ones holding me and I was not doing anything or neither did I have anything to hide. What could have made things go wrong in the house? When Dan and I or the children spoke with each other, we would talk about what was going on with them mostly and Dan would tell me in parables what the Canadian government was saying here in Canada and that he was working with them in Uganda. Dan also shared how Mahmood and Jebu were harassing him with threats. When I realized what Ansar was doing, I became more frustrated, and I was trying to figure out how I could talk to my family and not have my privacy invaded. Well, the Holy Spirit showed me another way I could talk to my family without the conversation being recorded, which was through Hotmail. Thank God for that! When I checked to see if it was being recorded somewhere, it wasn't. Thus, we decided we would continue to type some of our conversations through our email account so Ansar would not suspect anything, and we would still have his reading material ready for him. Late at night, I would sneak the laptop to call my family to do what we normally do every evening as a family, pray together. I knew the time and would call them. We would type our prayer, and my lovely daughter would play music and type the words of the song and dance like David danced for me together with her brothers. Temporarily, I had literally forgotten mostly everything, even the songs that we sang at night and in church. I would particularly memorize the Psalms. Some of them stuck out to me like Psalms 25, 27, 35 and 63 especially. I read through the book of Psalms over and over again because they resonated with what I was going through.

As the days went by, one evening, when Ansar came home, he called me as he would ramdomly do, sometimes just to try to get information from me or to accuse Dan. But instead He said, "I have your passport and not even your Prime Minister, what's his name again?"

I replied, "Steven Harper ..."

"Not even he could get you out of my hands."

I choked up with tears and said in my mind, *you don't know my God.* **With all of that I believed that God did not give up on me.** He thought I was crying because of what he had said to me, but that was not in the case. I cried because I knew the power of my God.

Ansar went to chew chaat every Thursday night (chaat is an herb that they chew and get high and sleep all day on the Friday). He came home high, crazy and frustrated. It was worst when he called me and started questioning me about the latest happening. He would start making up things. Accusing Dan of things, he had never said or done. At the time, he started communicating with Jebu and Mahmood again. They came up with fabricated theories of things that Dan never even told them. I was always surprised when Ansar told me those things, I had to go along with it. Then suddenly, one night, when he walked through the doors and called me, and demanded I call Dan and ask him for the contact information of the sellers in Uganda. When he was done rambling. I immediately called Dan immediately and told him what Ansar had demanded. Dan gave me the information for John in Uganda; he had no other choice.

    The next day, when Ansar contacted John. They talked and arranged something between themselves, but Ansar nor John mentioned anything to me or Dan about their arrangment. He was so arrogant; he did not know that he had no credibility with those people. Being the manipulator he was, he warned Dan again not to tell them that he was holding me hostage.

    After a couple weeks or so had passed, one morning around 10:00 a.m., after taking my shower, I had washed the few pieces of clothes. As I went outside to hang them out, (I had to pass through garage to get to the clothesline), Ansar came home for breakfast. While passing by, I noticed a gentleman sitting in the passenger seat of his car. I looked at the guy, he looked at me, and I continued walking. A few days later, I overheard Ansar's conversation on the phone talking about the guy. Apparently, Uganda had sent him as a representative to Djibouti to meet with him. I didn't know the gentleman's agenda, but Ansar really tried to impress him. He put him up in the best hotel in Djibouti for two weeks, wined and dined him while going back and forth with negotiations. But the guy came up with the conclusion that Ansar was still not able to purchase the merchandise, leading Ansar back to square one. I wandered why he didn't take that guy hostage instead and released me. After all, he was at his disposal, and that was the only way that he could have recuperated what they had stolen from him. As I said, I was the easy target. The mere thought made me angrier and more frustrated. Ansar retorted back to Dan and started putting more pressure on him than before.

    Meantime, I believed Ansar started getting more comfortable with seeing me around. It was now October, and Ansar had to go to Somalia for a week to handle some family business and left Luni in charge of me. Luni felt in good because she finally got to him. Remember, I said before they were only speaking French in the house. Her sisters came over to the house every day while Ansar was away to visit. One of Luni's sisters, who said she was a lawyer, was over that evening. She asked Luni in French, "Have you contacted the travel agency? Do you have her passport? Is her flight booked? Is everything ready for her?"

Luni replied, "Yes, and tomorrow night by this time she will be on the plane."

I pretended not to hear them. However, I got all excited, contacted my family, and told them the good news. My hopes were up, but that night came and went; nothing happened for a third time. Luni never mentioned it to me, and I did not say anything.

After a week, Ansar returned home. I was sitting outside at the front. When he saw me, he smiled. He looked a bit surprised that I was still there and asked me how I was doing? I said, "Good," and nothing else. He went in the house, and he and Luni went straight into the bedroom to talk. Apparently, Mahmood had finally sent them my return plane ticket. And Ansar had left Luni in charge of sending me home whilst he was gone, but she too had a change of heart like Pharaoh. God had hardened their heart. When they emerged out of the bedroom, Ansar looked very pleased with her decision. He turned around and looked at me grinning, but I pretended not to see him.

One evening, I decided to ask Ansar if I could go to the corner store to get toilet paper. I could not just wash as they customarily did; I had to wipe up first. He surprisingly said, "Yes." I was very surprised myself because Luni previously told me I would be raped or killed if I tried to go out by myself. Mind you I was one of the few people who was not dressing like them. I had gone with her for walks a few times, to visit family and friends who lived in the area and had seen a corner store as we passed by so I knew the route.

By then, I knew where I was going, which of course made me a bit nervous to leave their house alone, but I went anyway. I thought it was a bit of freedom for me. However, they had the guardian follow me. I went into the store, looked for my items to purchase, but couldn't find what I was looking for so I asked for someone's help, but they did not speak English. They went out and found a young American woman, who was familiar with the language, to interpret for me. She had been living in Djibouti for a while. A few days had gone by and I asked Ansar again if I could go back to the store. To get some ladies product. He said yes, and I happily left. This time, it was in the afternoon. When I arrived at the store, they sent to look for the young lady again to interpret for me. That same day while exiting the store the young lady said to me, "I saw you walking here before and you don't look well. What is going on with you?"

I said, "I can't talk about it."

She pressed, "No, you can tell me. Djibouti is a bad place, and I will help you to get out of here." I had met my third angel. I was scared and mumbled with my head down, "I am being held against my will." Then I walked away. I never told her who was holding me, or where I was being held. I then hurriedly walked straight back to the house because I didn't trust anybody at that time, I didn't know anybody over there. Also, I knew that the guardian was always following me, one of them in particular, who was the most loyal to Ansar and Luni.

I continued to go for walks as they would go to sleep in the afternoon. I couldn't sleep during the day, so they allowed me to go. One day I asked again, but this time in the evening, and they said, "Yes." That might have been on a Friday, because both Ansar and Luni were at home. I walked and walked until I couldn't see my follower anymore. He probably got distracted because they would meet friends on the road and stop to talk. On my way back, I met my new-found friend, we got acquainted, she told me her name was Tracy, but she still wasn't interested in finding out any more details about my captivity, and I was okay with that. She was just determined to help me get out of Djibouti. We started making an exit strategy, I told her I needed to get to the Canadian embassy in Ethiopia, Addis Ababa in order to get home because they had my passport. I kept asking to go for walks almost every day, whereas Tracy and I kept on meeting until we finally came up with a plan. I would sit under some trees in and around the area and wait for Tracy to show up. Nobody ever asked me what I was doing there or anything. The plan was to board the bus that was leaving to go to the Ethiopian border, where I would try to cross the border. I went back to the house and immediately texted Dan and the family and told them about the possible opportunity for me to get home. Tracy gave me her information to give to Dan for sending me money. Dan was skeptical. He wanted to know if I could trust her. Somehow, I felt that I could trust her. Somehow, I felt that I could trust her. A couple days later, Dan sent some money to Tracy through Western Union for me.

In the meantime, the next day, I checked online for a church to visit after being in Djibouti for almost five months. I discovered there were only three churches that was in the same vicinity of Djibouti; one Catholic, one Ethiopian Orthodox and one Protestant church. Mosques were not hard to find; they are in every corner of the country. I figured since the door was opened for me to go to the corner store by myself, I could ask to go to church now. I asked Ansar if I could go and surprisingly, he said, "Yes." I guess they thought they had nothing to lose by then because I didn't know anybody or couldn't leave the country. I didn't know the place, and they had my passport anyway. Besides, I had never done anything to make them feel suspicious about me. Luni thought I was dumb anyway, because I kept saying I didn't know whenever they asked me what was going on with the deal. knowBut I really didn't.

I was so excited to finally go to church after five months of not having any fellowship with other Christian believers. I had never missed church for such a long time.

The most I had missed was for about a week or two when I gave birth to my children. I grew up in church, my family has a church, and it's located just behind our family house in Trinidad. We always attended service. That Sunday morning, I got up, got dress and Ansar asked the guardian to call me a taxi. I was making my way to church finally. I was excited. However, when I arrived at the church, it was closed, even the gates where tightly shut. I waited outside the gates and eventually one of the gardeners came to see me. He opened the gates and took me to the back to meet with the people who was staying at the back. There was an older French missionary couple. They were very nice people, kind and gentle. They spoke little English. I told them I was there hoping to attend Sunday morning service. They said that the service was on another day, I think it was on the Tuesday. I felt really disappointed. However, I asked if I could see the pastor? They said the pastor was off, I will not be able to see him until Tuesday. They invited me in anyway and offered me some breakfast. While we sat and ate, I told them that I was in a delima in Djibouti, I was being held against my will. They wanted to understand me well that they really hearing what I was saying to them. They then called in a gentleman who spoke better English, I explained the story to him, but when I told them who was holding me, they were surprised. They said, "We know them. The father is a good guy. He brings bread and pastries to us every week and even gives donation to the church." Regardless, they believed me and showed me compassion. The gentleman even documented what I was everything I was saying. After I was done and ready to leave, they called the gardener and asked him to get me a taxi. I left that place with some optimism and hope knowing that I was going to go back and meet with the pastor on Tuesday.

    I did not stay very long so when I went back, I told Ansar and Luni that there was no service on that day, it was going to be on the Tuesday evening. They said okay. When Tuesday arrived, I was very excited to go to church. I even went a bit early because I was so eager to meet and talk to the pastor. When I arrived, the pastor ans I were the only ones there. We introduced ourselves to each other and I told him what was happening with me, that I was being held against my will there in Djibouti. He was shocked and said, "I don't believe you." I couldn't believe what came out of his mouth. I too was shocked, devastated and disappointed at the same time. The conversation got awkward, and we became silent. He then asked if I could stay for the service. With all of that, I did and I really enjoyed it.

    Before our meeting, I thought I was in my comfort zone because the church was the only place I had ever considered to be safe. However, the church congregation was made up of mostly American military families. You see, there are many foreign military bases in Djibouti: The

French, the Americans and other countries, but the sad thing was that there was not one Djiboutian congregant in the church. Service finished around 9:00 p.m. that night. It was very dark outside. I asked the pastor if somebody could give me a ride home. He asked a family the area that Ansar lived in and they were happy to do so. I could not help thinking that the one person I expected to believe me did not, <u>the pastor</u>.

     In Djibouti, everything shuts down from 12:00 noon to 5:00 p.m. and people went home for lunch and napped in true siesta. Then, they got up, got dressed and went back on their normal daily activities. I was not used to those customs; therefore, I could not sleep during the day. I used to go sit outside, read my Bible, and pray. Meanwhile, Ansar used to call me to the dinner table to eat with them every time. But After a couple months or so, I began to feel really uncomfortable and manipulated. One day I decided, no more. I was not going to sit and eat with them anymore. started telling them, I wasn't ready to eat at the moment. I just couldn't do it anymore. Also, I felt like I was being forced and that Ansar was getting more and more use to seeing me around. It was also agonizing for me knowing I did not want to be there and was forced to eat with them too.

6

ONE AFTERNOON, I ASKED TO go for a walk again. I kept passing a pay phone on my way to the cornerstore. I went in and called my friend Tracy. She wanted to meet with me because she had some news. When we met, she told me what time the bus left every night to go to the Ethiopian border. The walk had become routine for me. The following night, when Ansar and Luni went to sleep, I packed a few pieces of clothes in a bag and snuck out of the house. I went to the corner store and asked if I could leave it there. They were familiar with me then, they said, "Yes." They did not ask me any questions.

This was my grand escape or so I thought.

Meanwhile, Ansar had to go away for a couple of days, and I was left with Luni again. Finally, the day had arrived for me to leave. That evening, I told Luni I was going to church. I left the house and went straight to the corner store, picked up my bag, and met up with Tracy. She called a taxi, and we went to the place to catch the bus. When the time came to board the bus, Tracy led me to the bus, but she did not go on with me. I thought that was the plan, but she said she couldn't go. Terrified, I hesitated for a while, but I decided to take the chance. I was not going to let anything stop me. I had taken one of Luni's scarfs from the wardrobe in the room I was slept in. I wanted to cover my head in order to blend in with the locals. However, I boarded the bus. The bus left around 8:00 p.m. and off I went, on my way to the Ethiopian border. I was scared, nervous.

Whilst on the bus, I began thinking about what Tracy had said to me earlier that evening. She was a bit concerned for me because one of her friends told her that going through the border alone can be very dangerous. He said my life could be in danger. I thought to myself, how much more danger could I be in? My life is already in terrible danger. Apparently, there are thieves and violent men just waiting to prey on the vulnerable people arriving at the border, specifically women arriving at the border. Tracy was particularly concerned for me, knowing I did not speak the language or know the culture.

The army conducts check points on the road every so often. They would stop vehicles and ask for your passports or a certain travel identification. They even checked bags and would even take whatever they pleased.

But they did not ask those ladies for any documents nor did they search them as they did the other passengers. As for me, I was posing as one of those ladies. They did not check me or asked me anything, and I did not open my mouth to speak whatsoever. The bus was filled with the domestic women, I kept to myself and avoided making eye contact with anyone. The domestic women were uneducated and most of them had no passports. They would cross the border every day to find work and send money for their family. They travelled from country to country, all over Sub-Sahara Africa, risking the chance of being exploited, abused and ostracized by both men and women alike. This is a problem in Africa. The various governments know about the problem, but nothing is being done to make conditions better for them.

We drove for about three hours until we reached the Ethiopian border. Everything seemed to be going good so far. When the ladies started getting off the bus, I followed as they headed to another bus that was waiting there on the border. Suddenly, this guy came and called me out of the line and asked me for my passport. I froze; I did not know what to say. I looked cleaner than the other ladies, and I think that sold me out. He spoke to me in his language. I did not answer., because I did not understand, He spoke to me in English and asked me if I spoke English. I said yes. He then escorted me to a small building next to the border. I was startled, I did not know what to do next.

They called me to the window and asked me for my ID, and on impulse, I quickly pulled out an identification card that I had from Trinidad when I was 16 years old. I did not want them to know that I was Canadian because I thought for sure they will send me back. The gentleman looked at the ID, then looked at me. Of course, I didn't look the same. I was many years younger. Also, I was very thin and frail, so I really did look totally different. Also, I don't think they even know of the country Trinidad and Tobago. Immediately he instructed the other young man to take me back to the Djiboutian immigration. I had no choice but to just comply. I didn't quite understand what was going on.

When I arrived there, nobody said anything to me. They spoke French and Somal mostly. I was asked to stand aside and wait that somebody who spoke English. I stood in the corner waiting and waiting thinking what could happen to me next. There were people in lock-up behind the fences. I waited and waited and stood there all night. The person arrived around 8:00 a.m. the next morning. When she arrived, she called me and asked me where I was coming from. I told her Djibouti, She said, "You need a visa to go to Ethiopia, so we're sending you back on the bus to Djibouti. She mentioned the bus would be arriving around 11:00 a.m. The bus arrived exactly at 11:00, I boarded and headed back to my misery. At that point in time, I was okay with going back the place I was familiar with, Djibouti. Yes, the place where I was being held captive. That was all I knew for five months. I thought to myself, I could have gotten lost in that part of the world, and my family would never see me again, as Tracy feared. It was a very dangerous and scary situation for me.

On my way back, I kept trying to come up with some excuses to tell Luni. That was the first time I had ever tried to escape. Remember, Ansar had gone away on family business. The bus went directly to downtown Djibouti. We arrived around 2:00 p.m. I took a mini-bus and headed right back to the hellhole to my captures. Before I went back to the house, I went to the convenient store, where I left my little bag. I then walked straight back to the house. While I was walking, I saw one of the guardians. It looked as if he had been searching for me around the area. He started following me. I saw him from afar off, I did not turn around. I just kept on walking until I reached the house. When he saw me, he followed me straight to the house. I was really scared, wandering what would Luni do to me?

Strangely, when I walked into the house, she did not seem to be very concern that I was out all night. She asked me where I was, and I made up a bif story, that my friend that I went to church with, took me for dinner after and she couldn't take me back so I spent the night at her place. She believed the story that I told her. I was not expecting the reaction that I got from her. Luni did not care because she was tired of seeing my face every day, and at least she didn't have to see my face for one night. I knew God was with me all the way. Like Pharaoh, God made them believe the lie instead of the truth. You could imagine my family's disappointment. They were devastated when I told them what happened; I was more disappointed.

When Ansar got back home from his trip, he didn't say anything to me either. I'm not sure if Luni had already updated him. They never thought I would had tried to escape anyway. The next day, guess who called me? Yes, Dr. George. He asked me where I was that night and if everything was okay with me. He sounded as if he concerned, but he was asking for Ansar. All I said to him was that I was okay.

Meanwhile, I did not know then, but there are two Ramadan. Ansar left me at his sister and brother-in-law Omar's house when he worked nights. Luni conveniently went to her family in the evenings when he was working nights and she did not want to pick me up when she was going back home. so I had to stay there until Ansar could pick me up.

Omar and his wife pretended to be nice to me, especially Omar. He would ask me the same thing whenever I was at their house. "You wanted to come to Djibouti right, nobody forced you to come here?" I always answered, "Yes." What else could I say? Their house had two levels and was very secluded. When it got dark, I felt clusterphobic, I couldn't breath in that house. I used to go outside in the front yard because I felt trapped inside the house. I couldn't breathe. They also had a gentleman staying downstairs in one of the rooms. Omar introduced me to him and told me that he was staying there. But the guy was not speaking to anyone, he was just there. I did not quite catch the story. I was in my own misery. The gentleman did not say anything to me. Omar spoke for him, and he just went back into the room. He was probably in the same predicatment as I was.

One evening, Ansar dropped me off. He had to go to work. It was getting closer to Ramadan and he worked until 3:00 a.m. in the morning. Omar and his wife decided that should sleep over at their house. They fixed a bed for me. The room was very hot. I tried to be polite and lay down I couldn't sleep. It was too much for me. They called Ansar, and he picked me up. I felt like a yoyo not knowing what was going to happen to me from one day to the next or which way I was going.

Since the first fight between Luni and Ansar, his mother had told him to send me home. He promised, but as time passed, he never did. Whenever the parents went to the to visit them, especially his mother, she would ask him, "Why is she still here? You need to send her home." He kept saying, "Yes," but he did not want to listen to anyone. He couldn't because God was not done with him yet. Even Luni's mother pleaded with her to send me home, but she did not. Her mom went with one of her daughters to Somalia on vacation for about six weeks. When she returned and visited Luni and saw I still there, she was surprised to see I was still there. There was nothing different anybody could tell them to change their minds. They were already in too deep. They told me not to open the bedroom windows or go outside by myself, even during the day, that someone could kill me, or they could climb through the window and rape me.

However, a few days later, I had a third dream. I dreamt of my aunt Angel again. This time, she was in the same room as before, playing a game with a little girl. She she said to me, "They're playing games." I did not know who she was talking about. I woke up wandering who was playing games. I just couldn't figure out what that dream was all about, but I kept thinking my life was literally just wasting away.

It was almost six months into my captivity and they, especially Ansar, was getting more comfortable with me being around. Becase I was quiet and never tried any antics or trick around on them. I was not a loud person. I didn't eat up all of their food, and I never spoke back to them, that is not my personality. I did was to read my Bible, I prayed a lot, and cried everyday I was there. I just didn't know what to do in my situation. When I spoke to my family, it was my best time. All I wanted was to return home to be with my family again. I used to dream I was going to Montreal, and I would be driving on the highway close to my home.

A few days later, Ansar was talking on the phone. He called out to me and said, Dr. George wanted to talk to me. I was confused because he was casually talking, It dawned on me then to ask him, "Did Dr. George call?" He didn't answer; he just passed me the phone. Remember, Dr George was the Canadian Consulate. When I answered, he asked me how I was doing that the Canadian government wanted to know how I was doing. It was strange. I felt like something was not quite right. He didn't even ask to see me. I told him I was doing okay. That night when I spoke with my husband Dan, I told him what had transpired. I mentioned that I believed the Canadian consulate was working with my capturers. I reminded Dan of the previous updates they were getting about me whenever they spoke with the Canadian government. They were being told that I was doing well, when Dr, George never saw me. The following day when the Canadian government's representative called home, Dan told her what I said. She told Dan, "Tell your wife not to tell Dr. George anything about her situation anymore, or what was going on with her, especially, if she gets the opportunity to leave." She told them to tell me to leave everything behind if I have to and just get out of Djibouti. They had believed in me. I starting thinking about everything that happened Brginning from the first day I met him how he responded to my situation until then. I was not too happy with the him nor the Consular help he was giving me. As the Canadian represenatitve overseas, that should not have been the case. He was corrupted by Ansar and his brother-law. When he was supposed to be representating and helping Canadians in Djibouti. How bizzare.

    I was not happy about leaving my luggage with the thought of leaving all of my fine clothes and precious jewelry but I had finally woken up and said to myself, "It's okay. They're just things."

    I would usually fell asleep around 5:00 a.m. in the morning Djibouti time. Remember it was difficult for me to eat or sleep. One morning I was awakened around 7:00 a.m. There was a lot hustling and bustling around the house, even in the room where I was sleeping. The workers were frantically cleaning. They were pulling and pushing things around. One of the servants forgot the hose running in the bathroom, and the whole house got flooded. Luni had them wash the clothes by hand, sheets and all, even though they had a washing machine. There was a small drum in the bathroom, and she forgot she had left the hose running. It overflowed enough to fill up the house with about a foot of water. I didn't know I was asleep through the whole episode. However, as I mentioned before, Luni felt the strange things that were happening, was because I was there. She always cautioned Ansar. It was true, (hence the code name Pharaoh). Ansar kept his shoes in the room where I slept. Even though I was there for six months, you would think he could have moved his shoes, but he didn't. He went into the room every morning to get a pair of shoes for work. At the beginning, he knocked before entering. At some point, he stopped knocking and was just entering the room in the mornings. Sometimes, I pretended I was sleeping. Then, there were times I was sleeping and didn't realize I wasn't covered up properly. Remember, it was really hot, even at night it was 33 degrees celcius, so I would sleep in strappy comfortable clothes that sometimes ride up. I was very disgusted when I realized what was happening. He would condtantly tell Luni she was too fat, that she must lose weight like me. Mind you, my weight loss was not by choice. I was kidnapped and couldn't eat or sleep or even function on my own. Hence the reason why she felt threatened by me.

    I remembered one of her sisters went over to visit. When she saw me, the first thing she said to Luni was that I didn't look well. They didn't care. I could have died there, and they would have still believed that they were doing the right thing. These people do not regard people's lives as long as they get what they want.

    Luni's niece and nephew went over to the house one evening after school, and she did their homework with them. They studied in French. Luni put her glasses on and everything, she was looking all studious and acted as though she was a teacher too. Anyway, I was around just observing and listening on the side. Her nine-year-old niece was left with some work to do whislst she exited the room for a moment. The child approached me to asked me for some help. When I looked at the material, I recognized that some of the work that Luni had helped her with was wrong, so I corrected it. When Luni returned and heard me explaining things to the child, she didn't say anything. But on that day her eyes opened up. She then decided to take me seriously about my understanding of the French language. Remember, I told them at the beginning I wasn't fluent in French, but I read, write and understood it. I had done French up to college when I was living in Montreal. I was the one helping my children with their homework when thet were attending their French schools.

    After her enlightenment, whenever people went over to the house, she would tell them parle en Somali (speak in Somali) because they no longer wanted me to understand their conversations. As they spoke French all the time, especially too when visotors were over. That was okay for me because I started picking up on the Somali language too, which would come in very vital for me at some point in time. After that episode, Luni started acting a little more generous towards me. She had a small store downtown in Djibouti and decided to ask me if I wanted to go to work with her. I was happy to get out and said, "Yes." I went for a few days with her, but it was really boring. She did not get a lot of visitors in her store at all because she only sold foreign items, which was very expensive for most of the locals living there in Djibouti. I had come to understanding that for the second Ramadan, they boughgt the children new clothes and gifts. They cleaned up the house up and celebtated with family and friends.

One of her sisters had passed by the store to check out the new items Luni had brought into the store. She had taken other family members with her. They had become very occupied, at one point. I decided to ask Luni to go for a walk to look around. She said, "Yes." I took her niece with me. As we walked down the street, I saw a store that sold cell phones. We went in and checked it out. Since I had some money that Dan had sent me through Tracy. Remember by that time, they were giving me a little leeway. The next time we went back to the store, I asked again and returned to the cell phone store and bought a flip Nokia phone that suited my budget. The store was not far from hers. Anyway, I knew they would not have never allowed me to have a phone, so I hid it safely from them. But, I needed a SIM card to get the phone working. All the house workers used to live in and around the house except for the cook. She was one of the most recent help. She spoke a little English. Because Luni treated her workers so badly, they would always leave suddenly. They were always left in a pickle and they needed to hire new workers quickly. This happened very often. The worker would not show up one morning, and Luni couldn't cook, not for her life. They also had a big range stove sitting there, but the cooks had to cook the meals on a small one burner gasoline stove in the middle of the kitchen floor. This was for three meals a day. Anyway, the new girl would leave every evening return at 6:00am every morning to clean up the mess from overnight and make breakfas. When she was leavin in the eveningg, I asked her if she could get me a SIM card. I gave her some money. A couple of days later, she brought it to me. I was set. As I was going for more frequent walks, I had also been secretly talking to my family and Tracy while I was outside.

Meanwhie, the evening before that second Ramadan, as Luni and the workers were busy preparing for the next day. Around 7:00 p.m., the room where I slept in, started filling up with locust flies above the curtain head. It had spread all through the hallway walls in the house. They didn't understand what was happening. The workers and I had to through the house, killed and chased away the most we could. That evening Ansar brought home a couple of goats. I asked what it was for. Luni explained to me that they were going to sacrifice the goat the way Abraham sacrificed his son, take the blood, and put it on the walls. "I don't believe in that I said. Jesus

Christ already died for our sins, so we don't have to sacrifice animals anymore," She didn't say anything. A few minute later, all excited, she said there were special people who go around from house to house to sacrifice the goats. Those poor goats cried all night. I felt terrible for them, I guess they sensed they were going to be sacrificed. Everybody had at least one of them in their yards. It felt very demonic and dark to me. I did not know what to do with myself when I got up that morning. I just did not want to be in that environment. I asked Ansar if I could go to church, He said, "Yes." I went, but there was no service on that day. One would think on a day like that the church will be open and people would be praying for Djibouti during this dark time. At least that's what I assumed.

Meanwhile, as Dan was getting more and more desperate. He decided once and for all to John, the main gentleman who was in charge of the whole deal in Uganda, to finally tell him what was really happening. That his wife was being held in Djibouti against her will for more than five months now. John was shocked to hear that news. Dan said he felt horrible and started apologizing to him. He also said he never thought Ansar and his people were capable of resorting to those measures, kidnapping. They had gone way too far. He apologized to Dan again and assured him that he would seriously to do something for him to get me out of Djibouti as soon as possible. Things were looking up...Dan called Ansar and told him the good news. That John had a sudden change of heart. He was going to finally go through with the deal. Ansar was elated, he couldn't stop smiling. He and Mahmood and Jebu and gave them the good new.

But Dan did not mention to Ansar that he had told John about my situation. That he had kidnapped me and was holding me against my will in Djibouti. They thought they had done it all by themselves. That their antics had finally worked, but it was just God who was working in it all. It was not going to be over until God said it was over. Like Moses, they had to stand and see the salvation of the Lord, whom they did not know. My supernatural God.

During all that time, I decided to check my churchs' website. My pastor at the time, posted a call for a worldwide prayer vigil. The call was for people all over the world to be praying for twenty-four hours. She asked for believers every where, no matter where in the world they were from, to pray. Every half hour someone was supposed to be praying. I thought to myself, this is amazing. Immediately, I put down the computer, went outside and started praying. I said, "Lord I don't know who is praying, where they were and at what time, but I am in Djibouti and I am praying."

When I started my vigil, I couldn't wait for half an hour to pray, because half felt like three hours to me. I went outside and prayed like every five minutes instead.

The clock just wasn't moving fast enough for me. I used to pick up small smooth stones, pilled them up. And specifically, when I was praying, pelt them against the concrete walls and repeating, "I cut off Goliath's head." After a couple days of my vigil, I started remembering the songs that we used to sing in church, scripture verses. I took pen and paper and started writing down everything I was beginning to remember. specific quoting scripture verses. One of the scripture verses that came to mind was Luke 18:38 "Jesus Son of David, have mercy upon me." I started hearing from God again. The Holy Spirit was speaking to me. I could hear him speaking to me clearly and I was also listening. Prayer works. Even though I was praying and crying everyday for more than five months and things seemed to be getting worse and worse for me and my family, things suddenly began to change for me. I had found the keys to opening up the windows of heaven in my situation. Thank you Jesus!

    Mahmood did not waste anytime. He flew as fast as he could to Djibouti to join Ansar to, as they called it, "finsh the deal." I did know he was there. But that day of the second Ramadan when I went to church and there was no service. I hung around the area a little, took a taxi and went back to the house. Instead of going directly there, I dropped off near the corner store. I was walking and, who did I see in a taxi? Mahmood. I was surprised to see him in Djibouti because as far as I knew, he wasn't allowed to return to back to the country. I was confused. He was residing at a hotel close by. The next day he came over to the house for lunch. When he walked in, he asked me how I was doing. I said not very well. and stated it was very hot there in Djibouti, and I had developed a bad rash with the heat. I proceeded to show him the rash across my shoulders and neck, but he didn't seem to care. He just left and went inside the house. When lunch was ready, they called me in to have lunch with them. Remember, I had stopped eating with them. But I thought since Mahmood was there, and I didn't want to be rude. I went inside and sat at the table to eat with them. When were sitting around the table, Mahmood kept looking at me with a smirk on his face while he and Ansar were talking in Somali and Mahmood. I felt very uncomfortable. With all of that, I didn't quite understand why he was there in the first place. When we were done eating, Mahmood called me into the family room and closed the door. He than began accusing Dan calling him a liar. I asked him why he would say something like that. I tried to explain to him that Dan didn't know the people were going to do what they did. He said, "But he is responsible anyway." Then he got up and left the room. At that time, I felt like Mahmood could have shown a little more compassion, but that's the type of people they were, brutless. A couple days later, Ansar mentioned he was going to Dubai. He and Mahmood had left together for Dubai.

But God's plan was not their plan, and he was about to show himself stronger to me than ever in my situation. As the saying goes, the darkest time of the night is just before dawn.

Luni was now in charge again, and her family usually visited her whilst Ansar was away. Thus, she was in all her glory. I can tell you that God is working in different ways in every part of the world according to the environment and circumstance of that place, as shown in the Bible. The things I experienced in Djibouti were just like in olden times. In those parts of the world, you still see camels walking in the middle of the road, shepherds, desert places, sandstorms and donkeys pulling water. So when you hear of ridiculous miracles like the dead being raised and many other impossible miracles occurring in different parts of the world, it is true. I proved it myself.

7

IT WAS NOW THE MONTH OF November. Being in captivity can make you feel as if you are stuck in an endless loop. You find yourself getting used to seeing the same things and start becoming more aware to details with the particulars of this cycle. At this point, almost almost 6 months had gone by since I was a free woman. The temperature was hot as usual and the air was dry as firewood. This was a very eventful time in the household as baby Mika was about to turn a year old in a few days. As a mother, that was a very exciting time because your baby is trasitioning from a helpless newborn to an independent little person. Luni wanted to ensure that everything was perfect for her so she put together a list of things to pick up at the family grocery store located not too far down the road. As Ansar was away, Luni took me to the store with her. Feeling both nervous and optimistic as I tagged along to help with as she checked off the grocery list. When we arrived there, she recognized a familiar face. It turned out to be one of Ansar's sisters who was employed there at the time. Smiling and speaking loudly, she said to her "Yes, I will be sending her home on November 26th, just after baby Mika's birthday. I already have the plane ticket. You would think that I would be ecstatic to hear those words. Don't get me wrong – I would of, if it was actually true. At this point I had heard way too many empty promises from dishonest people to actually believe anymore. In fact, these pencil-written promises got me even more upset as I wondered to myself when it was all going to end.

    The days kept repeating themselves. And in no time it was November 16, 2011. This marked the 6-month anniversary of my captivity. I looked back at the turmoil I had been going through I had been going through for the last 6 months and could barely recall the single joyful moments that had brightened my days during my stay in Djibouti. I felt helpless, weary, broken-in in a position where anyone would lose hope – yet this nightmare was only going to get worse. Around 2:00 p.m., I heard a knock on the door. Someone opened it to see the guardian who was most loyal to Luni and Ansar. Without any explanation whatsoever, Luni called me into the meeting in the living room. I was confused to why I was being summond. Hesitant to go as the they became quiet. Luni's tone towards me was harsh and very direct as if she was an irate boss yelling to her employees. In what seem to be nearing hysterics. She demanded me to sit down. Confused, I sat there like a lamb waiting to get slaughtered. She bagan swearing and asked me: "What did you leave in the store? I was stunned, feeling caught like a deer in headlights. I did not think the meeting was going to be about me. Of course, this guardian was the loyal one, and somehow, he found out that I had left something at the corner store. I had no idea how much he knew, but Djibouti is a small place; he could easily have fbeen informed from anyone in the area. Luni continued on her tirade, questioning "Did you steal something from me? I want you to go and pick up the bag right now, and I'm going with you. Hearing those words filled me with absolute dread. How did she find out so soon? I wondered. I was flustered with emotion, but I did my best to keep calm while she was swearing and spewing accusations of anger. Not being one for confrontation, and definitely not wanting to start one at that moment. I took a breath and composed my voice before answering. "No I did not steal anything." Unfortunately, my response did nothing to difuse the situation. I said nothing more and alloed her to continue on. At one point she became so upset that her verbal abuse nearly turned physical. In that instance I was conscious of the potential harm she could soon cause me and knew that it would take a miracle to get me out of that situation. I desperately prayed for help. God my never-failing protector, stepped in and turned the moment into a stark reminder of who He is. Tight when I though I was going to be hit, the English speaking maid jumped in between and yelled, "Don't hit her". Unkowingly, she was used by God to protect me.

In the past, Luni had physically abused some of her workers. She thought herself to be above everyone. For the past six months I was there, she accused and slandered me, but I refused to let her get to me. Since Ansar was away, Luni called her younger over lunch to have lunch with them as she uaually came home at that hour. She arrived at the house while we were walking over to the corner store to pick up the bag. Luni had not said a word to me while we were on our way to pick up there. When we arrived at the store, I asked the clerk for my bag and they gave it to me without any question asked. As soon as we arrived home, Luni spoke accusingly and said "You're stealing things. Empty the bag. I want to see what you stole." I emptied the bag in front of her as it contained nothing but my belongings; a few pieces of clothing and sanitary items. Still intent in finding fault, she accusing me. "You were trying to run away- not until I get back my money." I listened carefully for any telling signs, but thankfully there were none; nor did she react as though she knew that I had already tried to leave before. Luni eventually calmed down and left me alone. I immediately went into the bedroom to find my cell phone the moment as an opportunity. I quickly grabbed it and made my way outside as discreetly as I could as I could. I attempted to call my friend Tracy, but the call wasn't going through. I didn't know why, so tried again. After a few attempts, I realized the SIM card was out of my phone. Condidering myself somewhat technologically illiterate, it took me a while to figure that out. You see, once Luni had called her sister over for lunch after the confrontation thanks to the informed maid. She had removed the SIM card and put the phone right back where I left it as though it was never touched. That was my lifeline; now what am I to do? I thought frantically, I couldn't dare ask to go anywhere to use a pay phone, that was entirely out of the question. I had the wherewithal to I never contact Tracy online -thank God- because Ansar was reading all of the online communications. I fely trapped, desperate and devastated. The only thing I cmyself to do was to pray. By the time I went back inside, it was around 4:40 p.m. I overheard Luni's sister when she called the guardian to the kitchen window and said to him in Somali. S advised him that Ansar instructed to make sure, not to let me leave the house. I guess he thought I would try to escape again, but I had no plan at that point in time. Where could I have run to? Ansar and his family were well known in Djibouti. Not to mention I had already attempted to leave once before, which did not work out well. It was getting dark, and I and began feeling increasingly more restless by the minute. I went around the house to the balcony and once again, started praying. During that time, Luni sister had left the house. The entire situation was very uncomfortable as Luni and her sister felt they had all the power in the world over me. Even the guardians were acting arrogant towards me. *They were ostracizing me because I was trying to run away, right?* Little did they know, it was God who allowed it to happen this way.

That same evening, Luni's friend came over to the house to visit her. As always, they pretended everything was alright and that I was happy to be there. I didn't know what to do with myself at that moment. While they were sitting outside in front of the house talking, I went to the back of the house, I continued walking and praying. Around 6:00 p.m., the Lord started speaking to me. I heard the *Holy Spirit's* voice clearly whisper to me, "You're leaving today." *I said, Okay, Lord, how am I going to get out of here?* The guards wouldn't let me out. Anyway, I continued walking and praying. I walked as far as I could get around the house and was checking to see how that was going to happen, trying to figure out my grand escape, I saw no possible way for me to get out. The place was surrounded like a jail; there were houses on both sides. In front was the road and at the back an empty lot. They were two houses on each side. In one house, there were two US military guys living there. They wanted nothing to do with them. They had never even spoken to them while I was there. On the other side was the president's nephew's house, they had never spoken to them either. Those houses were surrounded by high concrete walls and barb wire. Don't forget about the two guardians that were guarding their front gates. I concluded that here was no way out for me. Again, I said, *"Lord what am I going to do? I know I'm supposed to leave today, but how* am I going to do that?" Yet, I believed God, and I trust Him more than I trusted myself or man. *He is not a man that he should lie.* He said I was leaving, and I was leaving. Ansar was in Dubai making preparations for when the merchandise was to arrive and that was supposed to be soon. Remember a couple of days before, Luni had also told her sister-in-law she had already gotten my plane ticket to send me home on November 26th. They had their plans but in the midst of it all, God had his way of getting me out of there, *"Not by might nor by power, but by my Spirit,' says the LORD Almighty," Zachariah 4:6.* God had prepared a table for me in the presence of my enemies.

    Whilst Luni and her friend were talking outside, I went inside, snuck the laptop, and messaged my family. I told them, "I am leaving today". That was it. I also told them to call Tracy and let her know I was leaving. Then, I went back outside and continued praying and walking around the house. I kept wandering how I was going to get out of there. I remembered at that moment what the government official had told Dan to tell me, "Leave everything if you have to and just try to get out of Djibouti". Anyway, my life was more important than stuff. I went back inside, wrapped up one skirt, one top and a couple of underwear really small and put them in a plastic bag. Opened the bedroom window slightly and threw them out the back. I made sure nobody saw me. I then went to the back, pick up the bag quickly and threw it over the wall in an empty lot located the back of the house. Then, I continued walking and praying again. Around 9:00 pm that same night, I heard the Holy Spirit whisper to me again, *"IT'S TIME."* I immediately went back inside. Luni and her friend were now inside of the house. They were sitting in the family room. I went into the bedroom where I slept, removed only my wallet from my purse and wrapped it in a plastic bag. I held it at my side and walked right pass Luni in the hallway. She didn't say a word to me, and I didn't say anything to her. She never even noticed anything. The Lord had blinded their eyes at that very moment. It hadn't even entered their minds at that time what was about to take place. I just kept on walking and didn't look back. I was wearing the same clothes I had on earlier, nothing looked different. The guardians were in their place as usual, guarding the gates. But I didn't need the gates to be opened either for God to take me out of there. Because when Peter was in Prison what happened? *Acts 12:3-19 "Peter was put into prison by King Herod, but the night before his trial an angel appeared to him and told him to leave. Peter's chains fell off, and he followed the angel out of prison, thinking it was a vision."*

    I walked out of the door and went to the back side of the house, where everything appeared normal. I checked, there was no one around. I had never taken notice of this before, but there was an old portable air condition unit facing the concrete fenced wall. I had already thrown my purse over to the empty lot where I had thrown the other bag with a the few pieces of clothes. There was no turning back for me now. With the inclination of the Holy Spirit's guidance, I climbed on top of the unit, unto the wall, put my feet between the barbed wires and began stepping through it one foot in front of the other. It was like I was invisible, nobody saw me, even though there were lights all around and the guardians in front of the house and people all in their houses. Nobody saw me. I threaded very slowly between the barbed wires. I could feel my feet touching the points of the barbed wires, and they were bleeding and burning. When I reached the end, I thought I could have jumped down over, but it was too high. There were two pieces of iron planks hanging over to the other side. I held on to them and jumped down. I then looked for my belongings, picked them up and hurriedly walked out of there. It was like a helicopter landed and took me out of there. I never thought I had I in me to do something like that, but when

God is in it, all things are possible. At that time, I wasn't thinking, what if I had gotten caught? I went through the back where I had learned how to take cheaper transportation, the mini bus. I went straight to the place where I had been the last time when I tried to leave before.

When I arrived, I looked for a pay phone and called my friend Tracy. I couldn't reach her at the moment. I waited a few minutes and called again. After a couple of times, I finally got her. I told her where I was and what was going on, but she had no clue of what was happening. I had asked if my family to call her and let her know, but they didn't give her the message. Since it was a surprise to her, she couldn't meet me at that point in time because it was a bit late for her to leave. She said she would send a friend to meet me instead. My family also did not know what was happening at the time either. Even though I told them the plan, yet nobody took me seriously. They did not not know what had transpired tha day. Nobody believed I was really leaving. Crazy, right? How was that possible for me anyway? But God is the God of the possible. He makes the impossible, possible. When God is in it, you better be listening. After about 20 minutes or so, two young men showed up to meet me. I had met one of them before, he was Tracy's acquaintance. They immediately called a taxi and took downtown to find a hotel to stay the night. I was not comfortable staying downtown because I knew Ansar and their family frequented the downtown area regularly. I was afraid for them to find me. Therfore, we went back to the place we had first met. We found a hotel room there. It was no luxurious place at all, but it was a place for me to spend the night, and I was okay with that. It was late, so they put me up and left. I went in, cleaned up myself, and went straight to bed. At that time, I had no means of communications on me.

The next day, Tracy came to see me. She instructed me not to leave the hotel room whilst she tried to figure out a plan on what to do next for me. The hotel didn't serve food, and I had to somehow find food. I tried to eat at least once a day. I didn't eat much anyway so that was not a problem for me. That evening, I turned on the television and to my surprise, I found Christian programming. I was like, in Djibouti? I was so happy because for the six months I was there, I never thought it was possible to even watch Christian TV. Bishop T.D. Jakes was on, then Benny Hinn came on, then Christian music. I was in all my glory. I started dancing and praising the Lord. It was the best thing ever for me since I was there; I was starving for that communion with the Lord. I was certainly happy because that was what I knew. I ended up staying for three days at that hotel while Tracy come up with the grand plan for me escape the country without a passport. As the first plan didn't work. But she was determined to get me out of Djibouti as she had first promised. In the meantime, my family had not heard from me since the day I left Ansar's home. They were worried sick about me, even the Canadian government was worried. Tracy had suggested I not try to call anyone on the outside for fear of being caught. After a day or two of me missing, Mahmood, called my husband, Dan, and told him I his wife was missing, that I was probably dead because nobody had heard from me or knew where I had disappeared too. He told Dan, they were not responsible for me anymore. How was that possible, right? They were the ones who kidnapped me, and they were now saying, they weren't responsible for me. My family became more worried. They were preparing for the worse. The Canadian government even wandered if they had failed Dan and his family.

Tracy finally worked out a plan for me. She picked me up some traditional clothes with a head scarf to wear for blending in with the locals. I already looked like them, so I blended in perfectly. Tracy brought a young man with her. His name was Javed. She said Javed was going to help me now and left me in his hands. Javed called taxi, and took me to the the same bus place that I had been to before to go to the Ehtiopian border. There we lingered around for a bit. As we approached the bus, he decided it was too late to take the bus, that I would have to leave the next day. He said he would have to stay the night somewhere. We took a taxi and dropped off close to downtown. We entered a dilapidated building where he said his brother had an office and told me we were staying the night there. I was nervous because I didn't really know the guy. The place was empty, there was nobody around. I went along with him, but I was thinking, I didn't even have a phone to call Tracy. what if something was to happen and I needed to call her. couldn't call anyone. Javed seemed like a nice person. He spoke some English. We were able to communicate at least because people there hardly spoke English, everywhere you go, they mostly spoke Somali. We just sat talked. I don't even remember now what our converstion was about about, because I did not want to tell anybody else beside Tracy that I was being held against my will there in Djibouti, I was too afraid to do so. It was wee hours in the morning. I was tired and Javed we should get some rest. I was going to lay down on the couch when Javed decided to make a bed on the floor with the cushions on the couch for us to sleep on. I was very uncomfortable with that decision. I remained sitting on the couch but he pleaded with me to go to sleep on the bed that he made. I didn't go but lay down on the couch instead. Then, he asked me if I was tired and started squeezing my feet. I got really creeped out and told him, "Don't do that." He immediately stopped. I was afraid to sleep after that. I felt like he was trying to lure me. Around 4:00 a.m., he finally fell asleep. I then was able to get a couple hours sleep myself. Daylight came and

I was very relieved. He got up around 7:00 a.m. and told me he was going to get some food for us. I gave him money for that and for him to pick me up a bag so that I could put my few pieces of clothes in it to travel. He also wanted to get the bus tickets, so I gave him enough money for everything. I waited and waited. Javed was not coming. I was praying and praying. I became really nervous, thinking he had taken my money and abandoned me in that place. Around 12:30 p.m., he showed up. I asked if he had gotten the tickets. He said, Yes," that we would be leaving around 2:00 p.m. to go to the bus terminal because the bus was leaving at 3:00 p.m., that evening. Around 1:30 p.m., he went outside, called a taxi, and we went around the sides of the building to leave. He was careful that no one saw me. When we finally arrived, it wasn't the bus terminal but he had decided to send me by taxi instead. we had been to before. I didn't question him. I was just going with the flow assuming he knew what he was doing. I didn't know at the time, that it was all God's plan. The was about to go through a different border this time. That was going to be the place where I was going to get my miracle. It was going to be harder than anyone could ever have imagined. I myself couldn't have fathomed what was next for me. Javed asked me to wait under a store as he went to talk to the taxi driver. After they were done discussing, he then purchased some chaat, went and sat down at the side of the road and started chewing. After a little while, he stood up, called me and put me inside the taxi. I asked him if he was going too. He said, "No" and went back sat down and continued chewing chaat with his friends. I was nervous. I started sweating. It was a jeep. I sat in there and waited and waited until it was full. When I say full, I am talking about cramped and people even sitting on top of the roof of the jeep. There were about twelve people in that one taxi and at leat two on top. As soon as we left, I started panicking. I asked the driver to stop for me to make a phone call at a public phone booth. I was so nervous of going into the unknown. I wanted to call Tracy, but he didn't stop. He said he had to make one more stop, I would be able to use a pay phone there. You couldn't imagine my nervousness and fears. I was afraid of going alone, but it was my journey to take, nobody could have taken it with me. When he finally stopped, I got out and tried to call Tracy, but I didn't get her. I then somehow calmed down a little and went back into the jeep. We continued on our journey and headed for the border. After about an hour and a half or so, we arrived at a place that looked like a big house. The driver asked everyone to get out except for me and one older lady. I think it was for a before the border check in. After about 5 minutes or so, everyone came back in the jeep and we continued on our journey. We finally reached the border about half an hour later.

There was going to be a battle for my freedom. But the Lord was in full control. I had to act like David did when he was running from Saul. I had to do some pretending in order to get my way through.

As we approached the border, the driver stopped. A border officer approached the vehicle as everyone exited the vehicle. We had to take all our belongings with us. We proceeded to line up, everyone had their passports in hand, except for me. When the officer approached me, I said I didn't have a passport. He asked me again, "Where is your passport?" I said, "I don't have a passport." They pulled me out of the line, took me under a shed and told me to sit. Meanwhile, when everyone else was checked in, they sent them to the other side of the fence. I was the only one kept on that side. The border officer came back to me and asked again for my passport. I repeated, I did not have a passport. "What happened to it?" he asked. I told him it was stolen in Djibouti. He then went in his boss's office to relay what I had said to him. It was getting later and later and they didn't know what to do with me. We were supposed to finish processing and leave at around 6:00 p.m. that evening to continue our journey to Somalia. I was the only one delaying everybody. They could have left without me, why not? The Lord did not permit it. The rest of the passengers began complaining, but the border officers decided nobody was going anywhere. They all had to stay overnight at the border. I don't know where everyone slept but, as far as I saw there were no hotels or motels just a couple of little shops on that side. The border officer came back and asked me again for my passport, he was very pleasant. I gave him the same answer as before. I had lost it in Djibouti that I thought somebody had stolen it. He asked me how. I said I didn't know.

That night, the place was a buzz. They were busy up and down, discussion was going on back and forth discussing from the border to the head office. There were military guards all around the place. It was surrounded. They had some really massive guns. They looked very serious. After a couple hours, they moved me from the shed to the opposite side. where the military bunk was. There were no females, only male personel. I was sitting and waiting under a tree with my belongings. Remember, those small smooth stones I used to collect, I had a coupleof them on me. I took one out and was just holding it and praying in my heart. Those stones felt comforting to me. One military person, came and sat next to me and started talking to me. He was curious to hear my story too. When he saw the stone in my hand, he said, "Wow" and drew himself back. I wasn't sure what he was implying, but I was only praying to my God and asking Him for help. After we were done talking and theu guy had left, I got up and started walking across back to the other side to ask to use the washroom. One of the military guards looked at me, raised his gun and said stop in French. I slowed down, but then continued walking. He then charged his gun and pointed it towards me. I froze. The the border officer ran out and told him it was okay. He asked me what I needed, and I told him I wanted to use the washroom. It was so very scary; he could have shot me right there and then. During the time that I went to use washroom, they brought out a cot and set it up in the open under a big tree for me to sleep. As they stood around watching the border all night. I was terrified and literally shaking. Then my new friend asked if I was hungry. I said no, but he insisted I ate and brought me a plate of spaghetti and a drink. I don't know if they had ever encountered anything situation like mine before.

It was a long day, and I couldn't imagine what was next for my fate. I eventually layed down and fell asleep as I was exhausted and stressed from everything that happened that day and the days before. During the night, the temperature dropped. I woke up feeling really cold. Not was not sure what time it was; it could have been up 4 or 5:00 a.m. It was around 7:00 a.m., when another border officer came to see me. He was very tall. He already knew my situation and said, "I've been hearing about you all night, what is your story?" I told him the same story that I had told the previous border office. I didn't have my passport because it was stolen in Djibouti. He asked me where I was from. I told him, "I was born in Kenya." I didn't know where that answer came from, but I immediately decided to say that because I thought if you're African, they treat you differently.

Meanwhile they were going back and forth again discussing over my situation. When the supervisor came in that same morning; they tried to figure out what to do with me. It was around 8:00 a.m., when a military officer came and escorted me into his jeep. He said to me we are sending me back to Djibouti. When I entered in, the taxi driver was also in the military jeep. I didn't quite understand why he was also going to the Djibout border because his car was at the Somali border. When we arrived at the Djibouti border, they stripped the taxi driver of his clothes and threw him in jail. Then they told me to sit under a tree on a rock. There other people sitting around too. Off course I couldn't sit down, I was very nervous, I just stood there looking around at everything happening and kept praying. The went inside to meet with the Djibouti border officials. They had asked the taxi driver if he knew I didn't have my passport. He said, "No." But they did not believe him. He knew because Javed had briefed him and probably paid him extra money for him to get me over the border. Hence the reason why he asked me to remain in the jeep when we reached the first check point. Anyhow, the border officials did not believe him. I was wandering when were they going to send me back to Djibouti. Well, like the first time, I said to myself, "I'll go back to Djibouti and go to the Ethiopian embassy there and ask them to issue me a visa." Right; how would they have been able to give me visa? I did not even have my passport. How loyal were they to the Djiboutian government? Were they corrupted too like the Canadian consulate was? I couldn't leave by plane anyway, because Ansar had probably flaged my name at the airport.

8

AFTER A COUPLE OF HOURS of waiting in the sun, one gentleman came out and called me. He took me into a room where there were approximately eight older men sitting around a table. They sat me down and started questioning me. They asked if I remembered what date I arrived in Djibouti. I told them I didn't remember; it could have been sometime in October. I actually went in May. They said if I knew the exact date I had arrived in Djibouti, they could have checked at the airport and followed my steps from there. Djibouti is a small country, so they would have definitely been able to follow my steps. But as I said, like David, I had to pretend. They then sent me back out to continue to wait. The Taxi driver was still in lock up. Confused, I didn't know what to I continued the waiting game. It was around 11:30 a.m., when the same military officer that drove us to the Djiboutian border, came and escorted me back to his jeep. He said to me, "You're going back to the Somalian border." He then went and took the taxi driver out of lock up and brought us both back to the Somalian border. I didn't know how to feel at that moment or what to do next, I was all confused. It was the divine favor of God; He had softened their hearts. That was indeed a miracle. Do you know that a foreigner is not able to book a hotel room without their passports in Africa, far less to attempt to try to cross the border and get to another country in Africa? I was going to be sent to another country in Africa without a passport. I remembered the night before that officer was a bit hostile to me but afterwards he started being very nice to me. God is good.

When I arrived back at the Somalian border, the authorities were all waiting for us. They sent the taxi driver over to the other side of the fence where the other passengers were, and they kept me with them. My new friend (my 4th angel), Jack, from the morning was waiting for me. He sat me down, looked at me and said to me, *"I know you're not Muslim. You're Christian. Tell me the truth and maybe God will help you."* To my amazement, how did he know? Even though I had my head covered, and I was wearing their traditional clothes, he had witnessed a miracle, and he knew it had to be God himself. I would guess that nobody ever got taken back to one border, where they had changed their minds and sent them back to the other border. *God is the God of the possible, and he can use anybody he chooses, even a Muslim to help you in your journey.* He then asked me again to tell him my story, to start over from the beginning. He asked me how long I was in Djibouti. I didn't want to change my story, so I told him 3 months. I also didn't want to tell them that I was kidnapped in Djibouti, because I didn't know how they would react to that. Therefore, I stuck with my story. He asked me if I knew who had stolen my passport again. I said no. He left and went to the office. He then sent two young officers to serch my bag to see if they could get any other answer than what I was giving them. In going through my bag, they found my wallet, which I was trying to hide from them because I didn't want them to know I was Canadian for fear of them sending me back to Djibouti. They started going through my wallet looking to see what they could find to know more of my story. They discovered my Canadian citizenship card. The looked at me and asked if I was Canadian. I said yes, but I was born in Kenya. They took my card and showed it to Jack. Jack too the card and showed it to his boss as they stood in the corner arguing back and forth. Jack was making a case for me and after a few minutes had convinced his boss. I did not know what they had discussed but he came back to me and said, "you're going to Somalia. I smiled and asked him when I was going to leave. He said to me, *"Whenever*

God is ready."

As I mentioned before, everything shuts down from 12:00 and 5:00 p.m. in Africa. The place got really quiet, everyone had gone to siesta except for the border supervisor. He was very busy working on my case. He was relentlessly on his phone, people kept driving in coming back and forth. I was just sitting there observing everything that was happing around me. Wen it was about 4:00 p.m., he called me and the taxi driver into his office. He gave the taxi driver a letter to sign and asked me for my Canadian citizenship card. He took it, placed it in the letter, folded it, sealed it in an envelope, and gave it to the driver. I didn't understand what was happening at the moment. The supervisor then sent me outside to wait. Imagine the rollercoater I was going through. Meanwhile, the people who were in the same taxi as I was, gathered together and had a meeting. They wanted the driver to leave me there. He didn't have access to his jeep, therefore, even if he wanted to leave me, he couldn't. It around 6:00 pm in the evening and it was time to leave. I was a bit hesitant to go with the same driver because of what he had gone through because of me. But when it was time to leave, they called me and put me into the jeep. I don't know if some of the other passengers took another taxi and continued their destiny, but there were a few new passengers in the jeep. One of them was a young man with his father, they spoke French. I was very happy, at least there were people I could understand and communicate with. It was finally time to leave. Thank God, I was getting out of Djibouti after more than 6 months in captivity and too without my passport, (but God). It had been 4 days since I had escaped from from Ansar and Luni's house in Djibouti. Nobody, not even my family heard anything from me or know what had happened to me. I had no SIM card on my phone. I couldn't contact anybody. They were wandering whether I was alive or dead.

    The first thing the driver did about half an hour after we left was stop buy get food before our long trip. I did not know how long the trip was going to be. The driver said the next stop was going to beat at 4:00 am, for breakfast. I did not get anything to eat because the place was not up to my standard. I just got a bottle of water. Once everyone got their food, we left. I thought we were going to be driving on the highway or at least on the roads. The driver was driving through rough terrains through valleys and mountains; there were no roads. I don't know how he knew where to go; driving through the night with no streetlights or roads, but he ended at the destiny, for breakfast at a house in another country in the middle of the forest. We were driving for hours and hours. It felt daunting. I couldn't sleep. He stopped at exactly around 4:00 a.m., in front of a little hut in the middle of nowhere. They were prepared and waiting for us. When we arrived, everyone got out but I didn't. I stayed in the back seat of the jeep and one of the guys who was riding on the top of the jeep stayed with me. Man, if I had eaten there, I would have gotten sick immediately. By-the-way, I had diarrhea almost every day while I was in Djibouti, the food and the water made me sick to my stomach. After everyone was done eating, resting, and preparing to leave, I went out and brushed my teeth with my bottled water and then returned back to the Jeep. We started on our journey and drove for another 3 hours or so until we reached Somalia. We arrived around 8:00 a.m., totaling 13 plus hours of driving through the valleys and mountains to get to our destiny. If you had told me that I would have had to go through so much to get back home to Canada and my family, never in my wildest dream could I have fathom that.

    When we finally arrived in Somalia, the driver stopped the vehicle, summoned me out and escorted me to a white car waiting for me. My goodness, I was more terrified than ever. I was in another country, did not know anyone there and I was being escorted unwillingly into a strange car. Even though I didn't know why this was happening or who was in that car, I had no other choice. When I entered the vehicle, the two gentlemen at the front was very pleasant. One of them asked me "are you scared" I answered yes. He saod, don't worry, you are safe here. Even though I was in the unknown, just those words comforted me. But God, I was depending on him, and like a little child I was doing everything without even thinking then. All I know was that I wanted to get home. However, I immediately remembered my Canadian citizenship card. I rushed out of the car and asked the taxi driver for the envelope. He pulled it out of his dash board and instead of giving it to me, he gave it directly to the other driver in his hands. Then, the other gentleman in the car turned around and asked me if I was scared. I said, "Yes." He replied, "Don't be scared, you're in good hands." Well, that calmed my nerve down a little. Can you imagine? That was blind faith. They drove me straight to the Immigration building. When I walked in, I recalled the place was quite busy. It was also very clean, and looked legitimate. Someone asked if they could help me. I said yes. The border supervisor had instructed me to ask for Hassan when I arrived there. I did as he said, they said he was busy and he'll be with me shortly. In about a half an hour or so, someone came and took me upstairs to meet milkah. I had to wait in the hallway. After about 15 minutes or so, someone else came and took me in to Hassan's office. He was an older gentleman. The first thing he asked me for was my ID. I gave him proper ID, my Canadian health and Citizenship cards. He then asked me what my story was, which I am sure he was aware of, that's why they allowed me to enter into their country, but I guess he wanted to hear it directly from me. I explained the whole story to him again. I also added that my parents were from

Trinidad, but I was born in Kenya because they were missionaries there. During my questioning, a gentleman approached Hassan's office, he montioned for him to join us. The gentleman was from Kenya and Hassan was happy to introduce him to me. He started talking to me in Swahili. He said hello and asked me how I was doing. Even though I understood hello and how are you in Swahili, I had forgotten how to answer him. What an embarrassment. My mimd was all frazzled and confused. I couldn't remember how to answer him. I knew because Dan spoke Swahili with his family all the time; of course I knew the basic stuff. I felt like I was caught off guard. That was not the only thing I had forgotten. I couldn't remember people's names and phone numbers and many other things. I did not have any reality or concept of anything else but my surroundings and what was going on with and around me at the time. Hassan and the gentleman continued talking. When he left, Hassan said to me, "I think I'll send you to Kenya to get your case processed there." My heart began pounding. I was worried thinking to myself, I don't want to go to Kenya. I don't even know where Kenya was located. What did I do? O Lord, did I make a mistake by saying I was from Kenya? But God had me covered. There are no mistakes when He is in control. Hassan then asked me to wait outside. I stood there and was waiting and praying (my 5th angel was about to come in). While I was waiting outside

Hassan's office, four gentlemen passed me by entered his office. Hassan had kept my ID cards on his desk. As soon as the gentlemen walked in, one of them recognized my Canadian ID cards on the table. He asked Hassan if I could join them, that was really rare thing for those men to do.

We started talking, and a couple of them said they lived in Toronto, and Canada was a very nice country to live in. They were really excited to talk about Toronto. Then, they reverted to continue to talk to Hassan in Somali. When they were done conversing, and stood up to leave, one of gentleman said to Hassan, "Make sure you send her back safely to Canada, okay." Hassan reassured him, and they left.

Then, Hassan called his right-hand man, Arun, and told him to take care of me. Arun took me right away under his care. We lwft Hassan's office, he drove me straight to a hotel in the middle of downtown. The hotel was pretty clean, much bigger and very clean, better than the last couple places. I stayed in. When I was settled in, I went down and asked at the front desk where I could purchase a SIM card. They asked one of the workers to take me get it. I was very happy. My phone was working again. I was finally able to contact my family after five days on the run. When I called home and Dan heard my voice, he was elated, he said, "Is it you, Lynette?" I replied, "Yes it's me." He was relieved. He said, they were very worried about me. They didn't know what had happened to me or where I was, if I was alive or dead. I didn't even tell him what I had gone through during those five days since I had escaped, and how I made it to Somalia. My family were just happy to hear my voice and to know that I was safe and alive.

As soon as we were done talking, Dan immediately called the Canadian government to let them know that I was safe and that I was out of Djibouti. Right away the Canadian government contacted the Canadian embassy in Ethiopia and sent them a copy of my passport from their office and told them to send it to the Ethiopian embassy in Somalia. I was excited, I was about to get a visa to finally go to Addis Ababa, Ethiopia. Finally, right? But the process was not going to be that easy. It was Africa and things never go as fast as it should.

I had a good night sleep for a long time. I woke up early in the morning, I was very excited thinking, okay, I will go to the Ethiopian embassy, get the visa, and leave. No, in Africa, they don't operate that way.

It was around 9:00 a.m., when a young man knocked on my door. He said that Arun had assigned him to me and we had an appointment at the Ethiopian embassy for 11:00 a.m. that morning to get the visa. I got dressed and we went to down the Ethiopian Embassy. Mr, Hassan had planned to personally be there to make sure I got the visa. I didn't know who he really was, but apparently, he was the actual immigration minister of

Somalia. What favour? God is so good. Hassan rode in a special jeep, and had a whole entourage with him when he arrived. When he entered the building, they honored him. He spoke with the staff and explained to him why he had to pay the Ethiopian embassy a visit, it was to intervene on my behalf. However, they said they never received a copy of my passport. That they had checked their office but couldn't find it, so they couldn't issue me the visa that day. Hassan got up and left, he I was very disappointed. I was more disappointed. But, as I said before, this is how they operate in Africa. The immigration officer drove me back to the hotel. As soon as I returned, I called Dan and told him what had happen. He immediately contacted the official at the Canadian government office again. The person who was dealing with Dan and my family was the head of all the Canadian embassies and consulates in Africa. If she said it was sent, it was. Thus, immediately she contacted the Canadian embassy in Ethiopia again so I could go back the next day to retrieve of my visa. That night, I became seriously ill. I had developed a fever and really bad cough. I could not sleep all night. When I was leaving for Africa, I had packed some medications for fever, cough, and cold in case Dan and I got sick in Africa, but I had left everything with my suitcase when I was fleeing Djibouti, I also had a diarrhea from the food that the hotel worker bought me for dinner that evening. When the immigration officer came to see me the next day, I told him I needed medication because I was running a fever and had flu like symtoms. There was a pharmacy just across the street from the hotel, he took me there, we to get some medicine and I went back to my hotel room, took the medication and rested until I felt better. The following day, instead of sending the young man to buy me the food, I asked him to take me to where he had purchased the food. I wanted to see the place because when I was in Djibouti, I couldn't eat food from just anywhere, it also made me sick. When we got to the place, I wasn't expecting to see what I had witnessed. I expected to see a little restaurant or something with people selling food. It was behind somebody's house. The place was damp and dirty and they were on the floor. It did not appear to be sanitary at all. However, they were used to it, so they didn't get sick. I ran out of there very fast. There was a little casse croute attached to the hotel that was very clean. I picked up a sandwich there instead. When the immigration officer came to see me the following day, I told him I wished I could have some soup. He took me to another hotel across town, where most of the foreign guests were staying. The place was really clean. I ordered my soup, and he ordered food. It was really good. I did not get sick after eating there. I even ordered some food to take back with me for dinner.

9

It was now the fourth day, since I landed in Somalia. The officer came by early in the morning that day and told me we were going to try to get the visa. The Canadian government told Dan they had sent another copy of my passport to the Canadian Embassy in Ethiopia again and they had assured them that they had sent a copy to the Canadian embassy in Ethiopia the day before. When we arrived at the Ethiopian embassy, I was a bit nervous. I didn't know whether I was going to get through or not, I had no expectations. When we arrived, I asked the gentleman if they had received a copy of my passport this time. He checked on his desk and said no. I began to panic. Then, I calmed myself down and asked him if he had checked his fax machine. He told me to wait and called another office to asked them if they had gotten it. After a few minutes, he confirmed that he had indeed received it. He stamped the form and handed it to me. Immediately I started crying. I said to him, I had been in Djibouti for six months, and they had stolen my passport. They were very happy for me. I went back to the hotel and called my family to let them know the good news; I had finally gotten the visa. I was all excited to go to Ethiopia, but as I said before, things were not that simple in Africa. It would take a couple days to get to the Canadian Embassy in Ethiopia, and the channel in which I would have to take was not an easy one.

On that same day, around 2:00 p.m., the immigration officer came back to the hotel and told me that I was leaving. I was a bit surprised. I replied, "Now?" He answered, "Yes." I packed my few things in my bag. Dan had sent me money. I had purchased a few more pieces of clothing and a purse there in Somalia. I gathered and packed up all my belongings, and we headed for a taxi to get to Ethiopia, or so I thought. I was nervous because I was traveling to unknown again. I didn't know where I was going or how long it was going to take me to get there or what was going to happen next. Like Djibouti, you had to wait until the taxi was full in order to leave. I asked the immigration officer if he could find somebody who spoke English so I could partner up with that person on my journey. Lo and behold (my 6th angel) was right there waiting for me. This gentleman was standing by the store waiting for a taxi also. The officer spoke to him and told him yhat I was looking for a travel buddy. He said he was also heading to the Ethiopian border and that he would accompany me. It was like he was sent there waiting just for me at that particular day and time. He came and met me. Almost immediately, we struck up a conversation. He was happy to speak with me in English. He told me his name was Digla and he had lived in New Zealand for a few years. I told him I was going to Ethiopia because I had to go to the Canadian Embassy there in order to get home to Canada. And right there we started talking and getting familiar with each other. He told me that he was going to see his family. He had another wife and family living a couple of hours over the Ethiopian border, and he had not seen his family in a few months. He was familiar with the place, and I was content with that. We then went to the taxi. He opened the front door, and I sat in the seat. He stood there waiting to sit next to me, but there was only room for one person. As I said before, they pack the cars up with people to the max. So I pushed myself in to fit in the middle somehow, and he sat down next to me. Eventually, the taxi filled up, and we were finally on our way to the border of Somalia and Ethiopia. About an hour or so into our journey, the taxi broke down in the middle of nowhere. Digla said, "Don't worry, I will stop somebody, and we will continue on our way." It was getting darker and darker and we were stock. The place was very secluded. My goodness, I was scared out of my wits. How could the taxi break down in the middle of nowhere? And who was going to find us there? I thought. After about half an hour or so later, a vehicle was passing by. Digla flagged it down. We hopped in and continued on our journey. It was the same kind of terrain as when through overnight to get to Somalia.

We arrived at the border around 8:30 p.m. Digla said it was too late that the border was closed, so we would have to find a hotel and stay at, we would leave first thing in the morning. He then took me to get some tea because the temperature gets a bit cooler at night that I would need to get myself a jacket. After our tea, we went to the marketplace that was surprisingly still opened. I still have that jacket today, I kept it as a souvenir We then went to get food and headed to the hotel. What kind of hotel would I expect to find in at the border? There are usually not a lot in those places. I didn't know how he knew where to find what he called a hotel. He said he always stayed there. I followed him knowing he was familiar with the area. When we arrived there around 10:30 p.m., it was very dark. There was a little entrance before the the actual building structure. I couldn't see the place properly. We paid for our respective rooms and they gave us us keys. When I opened the door to the room, it was so small. It was the size of a small closet; I couldn't breathe. I immediately ran out of there and told Digla I couldn't stay in that room. It was too small. His was the same size, but he didn't mind. He then took me back to the front, I paid for a bigger room. That room was about two times the size of the other room. I felt much better, I was able to breathe. Then, they warned me that the electricity usually cuts off around 3:00 a.m. every morning. My goodness, the place was already dark; it was gloomy, and the little electricity was going to shot off completely too. I was scared; I couldn't sleep. Around 2:00 a.m., Dan called to find out how far I was in my journey. I wasn't sleeping when the lights went off. I was terrified; I kept turning on my phone to get some light in the room. It was pitch black; I couldn't see a thing. Around 5:00 a.m., I went out with my phone light and knocked on my friend Digla's door to wake him up, I couldn't wait to leave that place. He had told me that we would leave to go the border office at 6:00 a.m.

Digla did not open, he didn't even hear me knocking. He eventually woke up, came, and knocked on my door. When he knocked, I was already dressed and waiting. He took me and showed me where the Ethiopian border office was and waited for me across the street. Imagine for a minute, If I had tried to get to Addis Abbaba on my own not knowing where I was going or what I was doing, anything could have happened to me. I had never been in those parts of the world and never could have never imagined experiencing such unknown. But God had sent help (his angels) to help me along every step of the way. What a wonderful, marvelous God he is. I am alive today because of Him, I give him all the glory. I was scared because I didn't know whether I was going to get the visa or not. The officer was very polite. I gave him the papers I had received at the Ethiopian Embassy in Somalia; he directed me to sit down, he took my fingerprints and stamped the form and sent me on my way. Finally, I was relieved. I went to meet with Digla and showed him the papaers; he was very happy for me. We headed straight to the bus station, boarded a bus, that headed to a place called Jigjiga. It took about 3 hours to get there. When we arrived in Jigjiga, Digla said, "I'll put you up in a hotel and leave you there, and I am going home to see my family." Once again, fear crept in; I started panicking. I begged him not to leave me in that place alone. When did I get so attached, right? I had just met the guy the day before, but he was a real gentleman during our short travels, so you can imagine why I got attached so quickly. As usual, what kind of hotel would I expect to find in these places? It was run down and there was no running water. I went in the room and put down my little bag down, but I couldn't stay there alone. I went back Digla to begged him to stay with me.

    He continued to remind me that he hadn't seen his children in six months, and he wanted to go to see them. I asked him if he would go with me to Addis Ababa. He said he couldn't do it. Then, I asked him what it if I pay for him to go with me. If it was money, I could call my husband and ask him to send it for me. He said, "No." Remember, the guy didn't really know me, we were just travelling buddies. Anyway, he took me to get some food. After we were done eating, we went to purchase the ticket for me to leave the next day because he didn't want me to travel to Addis Ababa during the night; he said bad stuff always happened when travelling on the bus during the night. The bus could sometimes fall down the hills. But the place was going closed the next day, I don't remember for what reason. We had no other choice, we had to leave that same night. Therefore, he decided right there and that he would have to take the overnight bus with me, he was not going to let me take that bus alone. What compassion, God had put in his heart at the moment. I was excited. I purchased tickets for both of us and told him that I would pay for his hotel in Addis Ababa. He was okay with that. I had already paid for a hotel room in Jigjiga but I didn't mind leaving that. We went back to the hotel, I picked up my bag and got out of there. Thank God I did not have to sleep in that place. We just sat ouside and waited for when the bus was ready to leave. We left around 7:00 p.m. We rode all night until the morning, the ride was 13 hours long. The bus stopped a couple places through the journey. Digla had told me to put on my jacket on because the check stop military guards would stop the bus during the night and go through our bags, and they took whatever they liked from people's belonging. We arrived in Addis Ababa around 8:00 a.m. that morning. By that time, I'd been travelling for days in all kinds of horrendous conditions. I had worn the same traditional outfit all through my trip so I would look like the locals. Incase Ansar and his cohorts were looking for me, it would be harder for them to recognize me. I don't know if Digla realized that I was Christian or not, he never asked me, and I never said anything. When we were in Ethiopia, he just said that he hated the Ethiopians because of the way they dressed. What could I say, God can use anyone as your helper. He is no respector of persons.

As soon as we arrived in Addis Ababa, Digla and I went to find a hotel. We stayed at this really nice hotel. It was very clean. Was Addis Ababa ever different from Somalia and Djibouti? My goodness, Ethiopia was the total opposite. It was very clean. The people were more gentle. They spoke very softly, and there were no loudspeakers blasting Muslin prayers all hours of the day in my ears. There were a lot of Coptic Christians walking on the streets and attending church. They dressed in their traditional clothes and went to church every day. During our time of travelling the border, I trusted to explain to Digla about what had happened to me in Djibouti and why I had to get to Ethiopia. I decided to do so because he was very respectful and protective of me. When we were booking the hotel rooms, he asked for the room just opposite mine so he could keep an eye out on me. It had been about 9 days since I was on the move, trying to get home to Canada, and I was pretty exhausted. I was literally fearing for my life, because I knew that my kidnappers might have been looking for me. They had probably informed interpole when they realize I was missing and was thinking I was still hiding somewhere in Djibouti. The agony and fear was real for me. I had been through many lows, but in spite of it all, God was keeping me in His safe keeping.

    Bright and early the next morning, Digla and I took a taxi and went to the Canadian Embassy. I was extrememly excited. I thought I was going to go home on that same day. But as I said, things don't workduffernt in Africa. When we arrived at the embassy, they were still closed, so Digla and I decided to go get some breakfast. When we went back, there were lots of people lined up waiting to get in. Digla was not supposed to go in, but they allowed him in with me anyway. I was so happy to finally be at the Canadian embassy. The foreign affairs minister at that time, John Baird. They had a huge picture of him hanging on the wall. It felt good. We had to wait again to see somebody.

    Finally, an official came and me into his office. She introduced herself as the ambassador's assistant. She noted that she was the person who had been communicating with Ottawa, Canada, all through my journey getting there; and she was very happy to see that I had made it safe. She also said me they would have to issue me an emergency passport in order to get home. I did not know what an emergency passport was, but in order for them to issue me to one, I needed to get a visa. Then she reiterated, "Don't worry. You are safe here." I was still wearing the Muslim traditional clothes and head covering. Suddenly, it dawned on me I didn't have to wear those clothes anymore. I no longer had to disguise myself. The next morning Digla took me to the visa office to get my visa. He was a travelled man he knew where everything was. When we arrived there, there were a lot of people lined up waiting to apply for a visa. Although not everyone got one. We waited all day, but I didn't even get the chance to see an official on that day. We had to return the next day. We got up bright and early in the morning and headed off to the visa office again. I was nervous and unsure whether they were going to issue me one or not because so many people were being refused. Thank God, they issued me the visa with no problem. I was very happy. The following day, I went back to the Canadian Embassy and showed them the visa. They could now issue me the emergency passport. They gave me some papers to fill out where I had to provide some relevant information. It was like applying for a regular passport. I had to provide references, take pictures, and more. I couldn't remember anybody's name or telephone number. I looked into my wallet and found couple of business cards of people who I knew and and gave them as refences without even asking. I had to even call home in panick to get another reference. The next day, I was finally issued my emergency passport. Thank God! That was more nerve racking for me. I informed my family. Meanwhile, they had already arranged to send the money for my plane ticket through the Canadian government in Ottawa so that they could send it directly to the Canadian embassy in Ethiopia. On that same day, the ambassador's assistant booked my flight. The flight was from Addis Ababa to Istanbul Turkey and then to Canada. Thank you Jesus, my flight was finally booked. I was scheduled to leave on November 31, 2011, and I was going to be home on December 1, 2011, exactly six and a half months since I left home. What a thrill!

    I was so excited. When I went back to the hotel, I told the hotel manager the good news. Digla and I went shopping that same day. I picked up a new outfit to travel in and some gifts for my family.

10

It was now Saturday, I was in a new country and felt freer that I had in the last six months and I felt as if the shakles and barriers holding me back were almost removed. I wanted to go to church to not only worship Jehovah Jireh but I also wanted to be in fellowship with my brothers and sisters. I asked the hotel manager if there were any churches around that I could attend. He said, "Yes." One of the staffs would take me in the morning. That Sunday morning, I was free to go to church. It was an imaginable feeling, just being in the house of the Lord. The young man escorted me to the church which wasn't far from the hotel. I arrived at this place that looked like a wooden abandoned shack. There was a lady waiting for me at the door. She was dressed in all white and had glamorous jewelry on. She was presented to me as my interperator as they only spoke Amharic at the church. She then guided me into the church and this abandoned looking structure came alive. It was beautifully decorated with flowers and wooden pews. There were also long red curtains running across the background of the pulpit. It was a rocking house and I knew the spirit of the Lord dwelt in this place. The presenter escorted us 0straight down the aisle and had me sit at the front row. The service had already begun and the had already started to sing and It sounded like heaven! They sang a song a song in Amharic and although I did not know what they were saying, I could that they worshiping God with all their heart. When the choir was done singing, a gentleman walked down the aisle praying for the congregation. He made his way down, stood up front, and continued praying. Then, he suddenly stopped. Approached me and began speaking to me in Amharic. He said, "I rebuked the spirit of death on you." I had never met him before. How did he know? A little while later, he came back to me and said, "I cancel that generational curse that came down on you." I was amazed, thinking, I had never met him before, how did he know about me? So, After the service, I asked my interpreter if I could go to see him. I asked that very question I was thinking and He said to me, "The curse came from your mother, but don't worry it is gone now, and you will go back home to your family in Canada." I was speechless. How did he know? I really wanted to bless church so I considered giving the little money I had but I was at a crossraods. My willingness to give trump by the incident that happened with the pastor in Djibouti who didn't believe me when I told him that I was being held against my will. That stopped me from giving to this church, but I believe God will give me another opportunity to go back to Ehtiopia.

I was about to face the scariest moments of my life before I finally left Ethiopia to go home back to Canada. *The battle was not quite over yet.*

it was Monday November 31, 2011. The day had finally come for me to leave that part of the world and go home. I was on the run for my life for two weeks and it was finally time for the fear, agony, and despair that I was going through would finally coming to an end. What a miracle. Thank God, I couldn't believe it.

But, I had to go through the drama until the very last minute. The devil was trying his best to cripple me with fear: I got up that morning, very happy and even more exited. Digla and I had planned everything. We had really built a good relationship and at that point I knew I could trust him. The plan was drop me off at the airport at around 10:00 p.m. that night and board the plane at 1:00 a.m.

I had about 10 hours to spare so that that day, Digla had decided to take me and show me around downtown Addis Abba. We took a taxi, went on our way. While in the taxi, Digla received a phone call. Throughout the conversation, he kept repeating the names of my capturers, Ansar and Mahmood. I got so scared; I started shaking. I didn't say anything to him because I had never told him the names of my capturer's, just that they were from Djibouti. I thought for sure they were coming to kidnap me again. As you could imagine, I got paranoid. I didn't know what that was all about, but to me, it sounded like he was planning something or something was in the works. I couldn't believe my ears. I said to myself, no way was this really be happening. I was trusting this guy all that time. However, I remained calm. We walked a little, got something to eat and left. As soon as we got back to the hotel, I went in directly in my room, called my husband Dan and told him what had transpired in the car. Right away, Dan contacted the Canadian official that was handling my case. She had assured my family they had unlimited access to her, they could call her anytime. She told Dan to tell me to call Canadian ambassador's assistant in Ethiopia to let her know what had happened. Because of my situation, I too was able to call that person at any time. In speaking with her, she asked me if I could talk to someone at the hotel about it. I said, "Yes." She advised me to let them know what was happening. I went and spoke to the owner/manager of the hotel. The whole staff was very fond of me. I would always go down and chat with them. They used to ask me things about Canada. Even the house manager was personally preparing my meals for me because I didn't like the food that they served at the hotel's restaurant.

The owner suggested I leave earlier than scheduled and not to tell Digla about it. I agreed, but I thought to myself, I couldn't do that. After all, he had done so much for me. I went back up to my room and started packing my few things. Around 6:00 p.m., I had built up enough courage to tell Digla I had changed my scheduled time and was leaving earlier to go to the airport. I asked him if he still wanted to drop me off? He said no. I then thanked him for helping me by giving him most of the Ethiopian money that I had. He was quite happy with that. I didn't want to make him suspicious, and he never asked me why I was leaving early.

The hotel manager quickly arranged for their personal taxi driver to pick me up and take me to the airport. They planned everything for me. It was agonizing for me. I was still nervous. I was thinking; what if Ansar and his cohorts were at the airport waiting for me. When I arrived, I kept checking my surroundings and looking over my shoulders to see if my anyone was following me. I thought, what if they came and got me? I was still in fear all the way coming home. Since I was early at the airport, I waited and waited and made sure that I was always amongst people. Around 10:00 p.m., I went upstairs and got something to eat. Then I went through the duty free, where I picked up a few souvenirs to bring home.

Finally, the time had come for me board the plane. I was exhausted. I slept through the flight. We arrived safe and sound in Istanbul Turkey the next morning. While in Istanbul, I was still nervous, I kept looking around my sorroundings, thinking these people could still try catch me and take me back to Djibouti. I felt as if people were following me all the time. I never felt safe. I was praying and praying. I trusted God to take me home. He did and is still able to make the impossible. Possible.

I had to wait for a few hours to finally board the plane for Canada. It was a long flight from Istanbul to Toronto, and it felt longer than it should. I couldn't sleep during the flight. I was just sitting there numb. I couldn't believe, after six and a half months, I was actually going home. I was on the run for my life for the past two weeks trying to get home to my family in Canada and it was actually happening. Thank God, I was finally on my way home. I couldn't sleep during the long flight. At one point I started searching for something inspirational to look or listen to. I had found an inspirational playlist of songs. Leona Lewis Footprints in the sand was on that list. How perfect. That song was really timely for me and for my current situation at the time, it really ministered to me. I listened to the song over and over again. When the pilot announced we were almost in Toronto and instructed us to put away our headphones, I didn't even hear. I was just lost in the words of the song. The flight attendant had to tap me on my shoulder to tell me we were raedy to land that I had to now put my headphones away. What a faithful God, He said in word in 2nd Timothy 2:13 "Even if we are faithless He remains faithful."

Finally, I arrived in Canada. I was home. The first thing I had to do when I met with the immigration officer at the airport, was surrender my temporary passport and then go through customs. The customs officer asked me how long I was away, I said six and a half months. He then asked, "Where is your luggage?" I showed him the little duffle bag. He asked if I was sure that that was all the luggage I had. I said yes. Then I said to myself, If you only knew what I had been through, you would not have even asked me that question. My God.

When I finally went outside the lobby, my family were waiting for me with flowers in hand. I was so happy to be home. I didn't know how to feel, whether I should laugh or cry. I couldn't believe that I was home. We hugged each other and left. The next day, Dan called the Foreign affairs office in Ottawa to let them know I had arrived home safely. Everyone in the office started clapping and rejoicing. Praise God for that!

As you could imagine, it was difficult for me to function normally for a long time after everything I had been through. I couldn't sleep because I was still very traumatized. I hid in the house all day. I was afraid to go anywhere by myself even though my family was encouraging me to do so. However, an incident happened three days after I arrived home. My son decided to take me for a drive that evening to pick up my daughter from choir practice at church. We parked in front of the church as we waited. While we were waiting in the car for her, Jebu's wife came out of the church's door. She stood not too far from our vehicle and was just staring at us. I thought she was looking directly at me, so I raised my hand up and waved to her as to say hello. When I did that, she walked closer up to the car to see who it was. When she realized it was me, she screamed out, "Oh my God." It was like she had seen a ghost. She didn't know what to do, she said, "Wait right here. I'll be right back." Apparently Jebu was inside the church, Minutes later, she and Jebu both emerged. He too was shocked to see me because they had no idea what had happened to me. Jebu did not say anything to me, he just stood there staring at me. I started panicking because they were the last people I wanted to see. I was mad at myself for letting that happen so soon. I did not want them to know I was in Canada yet because I hadn't yet figured out how I was going to reveal myself to anyone out there far less Jebu and Mahmood. But after praying for a couple of days I realized that God had allowed it to happen that way. When my daughter eventually came out, we left. After that event, I became more afraid and insecure. I felt really vulnerable.

On the Sunday my family and I went to church;

After the service, everyone was saying hello to me. Jebu also tried his best to talk to me, but I didn't talk to him nor his family. My children, especially my boys were very angry with him. They wanted to hurt him for what he had done to our family. But I told them no; just leave them up God, He would take care of it. A couple weeks later, our church offered an inner healing program. My family and I went through it and that helped. Especially my children to understand more of how to go about dealing with the situation. I had chosen forgiveness instead of vengance. Yes, I forgave them, all of them. I chose to cling to the scripture verse in Romans 12:20, "*Do not take revenge, my dear friends*, but *leave room for God's wrath, for it is written: "It is mine to avenge; I will repay,"* says the Lord. This was and still is my motto today.

 A few days later, my pastor at the time, called and asked to see me. He said he wanted to see me in the flesh. But apparently, he and Jebu had spoken in those few days. Dan and I went to see her together. When we started our conversation, he was very at angry at Dan, she told him; if he couldn't handle the game, to get out. I was confused, why did she speak to my husband in that manner? He had been through so much already. But before we went, I was warned that Jebu had tried to disqualified Dan to get him to dispelled us from the church. We had nothing to hide because we didn't do anything wrong. He however, stopped short of doing so. We kept attending the church because Our children grew up in that church. We however left a couple years ago and we had been attending for almost 15 years. When I first arrived home, for about a month or so, as I went to sleep at night, I would get up drenched in sweat because of the trauma. I had to change my clothes at least three to four times during the night. One night, I woke up to change. And after changing and had gone back to bed. While falling back to sleep, my daughter walked into our bedroom. I saw her coming in, but I did not remember anything else. She said she placed her hand on my forehead prayed for me. I did not remember anything. She said, when she put her hand on my forehead, I sighed and went right back to sleep. After that, I never woke up during the night with tremor and night sweats again. The next day she told me that the Holy Spirit woken her up and told her, *"Go and pray for your mom."* Since then, I've been sleeping well. I used to also dream about my capturers all the time. The dreams were all in Djibouti. That went on for months. I wanted to talk to someone about it; but I didn't know who I to talk to. I couldn't even talk to my pastor at the time about it. After what had happened when we went to see him the last time. I kept praying and praying about it. After a while it stopped.

With all the trauma and stress that I had been through, I started bleeding heavily. I went to the doctor to get it checked out. After many tests, I found out that I had developed fibroids in my stomach. They were as big as grapefuits. I tried everything to get rid of the relentless pain, But ended up having surgery to do surgery in 2013. It took me a long time to recover from that surgery. I had to take baby steps for everything. I was still recovering from all I had been through. I had lost and forgotten so much. When I tried to do normal things to get back to functioning into real life again, I would break down and cry. It was very difficult for me. Sometimes when I tried to go out by myself, I would forget where I was and just burst into tears. It took a few years for me to integrate in to normal life again. But one thing I did not and would not do; is make what happened to me, take over or cripple my life. With God's help and the help of my family, I have been going through life as normal as I could. I am doing well now by the grace of God. My belief is that, I came from God and have overcome all and that "He who is in me is greater than he who is in the world" (1John 4:4).

    My husband Dan has been battling some health issues since the tragedy. I must say, it did take a toll on him. He had been hit very hard. He was helpless during this period. Just imagine, your loved one being kidnapped half way around the world, and there was nothing you could have done to help or bring your loved one home. He had tried in every way he could to get me back home. kept hitting brick walls for more than six months. What was he to do? Thank God for his miracle working power.

Nonetheless, the children and I have been taking care of him. As the years go by, things keep getting more and more bleak for Dan's health, but we are praying everyday for healing for him. By God's grace, we know that he will pull through. We believe he will be healed in Jesus name. The battle is not over till it's over. God is God of the possible. We are going through this together. I am doing my best to care for him.

After I left Djibouti and came home, I had never spoken to or tried to contact any of my capturers both here in Canada or in Djibouti. As far as I know, nothing was done nothing was done to anyone of my capturers in my case. I didn't know that they, especially the ones from Djibouti, had the privilege to travel in and out of Canada as they pleased. Dan had given all of their names to the Canadian embassy in Nairobi Kenya. I thought the embassies shared information and my captureres would at least been flagged when they tried to enter Canada. Also, Mahmood and Jebu, they are just living their lives as normal her in Canada. No reparation was done for their behavior.

Dr. George, the Canadian consulate in Djibouti. He is still active there in representing the office of the Canadian govenment there in Djibouti. I don't know if he was ever reprimanded for his role in my kidnapping. After all, in all fairness. if he is corrupted and the government of Canada is aware of that. why is he still operating in the roll of the

Consulate general of Canada anywhere?

After all the trauma that I had been through. As I returned back to Canada. I had hopes that they would have tried to reach out to me in some way to help me to navigate life back to normalcy. But unfortunately, there was no help. Unill today, it is hard for me to even sleep as I am going through this book to make sure events were accurate after editing. However, I strongly believe that God is my defense, and my strong tower; He is still on the throne and He is the only one that's keeping and proctecting me.

How bizarre. In 2016, as I was still trying to heal with the writing this book. I was I was trying to put this ordeal behind to just with my try to go on with my life the best way I could here in my home country of Canada. Exactly 5 years to date after I escaped had from my captureres, on the exact anniversary date November 16th 2016. Dan had to go to a doctor's appointment on that day. After the appointment, on our way home, we stopped off at the shopping mall in my hometown to meet with a friend. Who did I bump into? Yes, Ansar's mother and sister. Both of them were walking freely in the shopping mall. As they headed towards me. I kept looking at the sister and her at me. I thought to myself, she looks familiar, but I could'nt recall where I had seen her. As they drew closer, she approached me and said, "Were you in Djibouti?" I said, "Yes." When I heard her voice, I immediately realized who she was. It was the same sister that Ansar used to tag team with to watch me when he and Luni couldn't watch me; Omar,'s wife. The same brother-in-law that as at the Canadian consulate general's office waiting for us when I had first met with him. I literally started shaking. I was shocked to see them in my own back yard. I felt very violated and threatened. I didn't know what to do at that moment. All shaken up, I just stood there. I couldn't believe I would have ever seen those people again. I just couldn't stop seeing their faces and hearing their voices in my mind. I didn't know what to do at the spur of the moment. I got all confused. Dan and I were just standing there and looking at them as they walked away and went to the other side of the mall. When they came back and I was still standing there. They did not say anything to me again. When we finally left the mall, called my sister Geena and told her. When I got home, I also called my oldest sister, who resides in the United States, and told her what I had just witnessed also. I didn't know who to talk to again. Dan and I were also preparing to leave to go to my uncle's funeral in the United States the very next day. Whilst we were on the trip, I couldn't stop thinking about those people. The memories started flooding through my mind all over again. I began to cry nonstop. When we returned home to Canada after a couple days, I called a family friend and told him what had happened. Still crying and all shaken up. He advised me to call the Foreign Affairs department of Canada and inform them of what had happened. They advised me to go to my nearest police station and file a report. I did. The reporting officer asked me; after getting back from DjiboutiI if I had ever reported the incident? I told her no. She asked me why did it take me five years to file a report. I explained to her that I didn't think that I would ever see my capturers again because I was supposed to be safe in Canada, my own country. She took the report and told me that another department was going to contact me, but I never heard from anyone again. It had been and still is a rough and trying time for me and my family, but we choose to dwell on the goodness of God. I choose to be grateful for what he has brought me through since I was a child until now. For God promised in His word, "I will never leave you nor forsake me." I felt victimized and traumatized all over again. I cried for weeks after those people triggered my fears and trauma all over again. The feelings eventually subsided and I continued on with some normalcy again.

My husband Dan has been battling with some health issues since the tragedy. I must say, it did take a toll on him. He had been hit very hard. He was helpless during this period. Just imagine, your loved one being kidnapped half way around the world, and you couldn't do anything to save or bring your loved one home. He had tried every way he could to bring me back home, but kept hitting a brick wall. What was he to do? Thank God for his miracle working power. Nonetheless, the children and I have been taking care of him. As the years go by, things look more and more bleak for Dan's health but we are praying everyday for healing for him. By God's grace, we know that he will pull through. He will believe he will be healed in Jesus name. The battle is not over till it's over. He's the God of the possible. We are going through this together. I am doing my best to care for him.

It took a while for my children to get back on their feet, but by the grace of God, they are all doing well. Our youngest son is in University abroad and, will be graduating soon. My daughter is also abroad, finishing up her studies at Hillsong College in Austrailia, and our oldest boy is also doing very well here in Canada.

I built up enough courage and strength to continue on with my life. It took me more than two and a half years after that to continue writing this book. I was too traumatized to start going through my ordeal again. However, with God's grace and the help of my family and this person who I now consider a friend, I conjured up enough courage and stamina to finish this book. I pray this book will bring encouragement and hope to all who read it. Be blessed!

Thank you, Abba Father!

ABOUT THE AUTHOR

Lynette was born in the Caribbean country of Trinidad and Tobago. She moved to Canada in her early twenties where she met her husband Enock in 1988 in Montreal Canada and got married a couple of years later. Together, they have three children, Sharnelle, Kevin and Andisson. She never considered herself to be a strong person mentally and physically, but by God's grace, love and mercy, she is an overcomer. She practically grew up in the church and is a strong believer in Jesus Christ. She has been through difficult life struggles streaming from her mother dying when she was only seven years old. But nothing prepared her for what she went through in 2011. This book was a great accomplishment for her. It took her 4 years to finally complete and her hopes are that many people will be blessed and encouraged by reading her book so that they too can trust and believe that the God in which we serve is the God of the possible, nothing is impossible for him.

www.ingramcontent.com/pod-product-compliance
Lightning Source LLC
Chambersburg PA
CBHW071118160426
43196CB00013B/2613